Bikepacking in the Lake District

Lakeland 200 and seven long-weekend bikepacking adventures

by Ed Hunton

JUNIPER HOUSE, MURLEY MOSS,
OXENHOLME ROAD, KENDAL, CUMBRIA LA9 7RL
www.cicerone.co.uk

© Ed Hunton 2023
First edition 2023
ISBN: 978 1 78631 117 7

Printed in Turkey by Pelikan Basim using responsibly sourced paper.
A catalogue record for this book is available from the British Library.
All photographs are by the author unless otherwise stated.

Route mapping by Lovell Johns www.lovelljohns.com
© Crown copyright 2023 OS PU100012932.
NASA relief data courtesy of ESRI.

For Tilda, with love

Acknowledgments

To John Spurr who sent me packing to Greece on an old Kona; the 6am crew who help keep me in shape; Tom and Lucie who rose to the challenge and carried me with them; Kieron Chissik, a truly inspiring backwoodsman and artist; and to my partner, Nicky Stoupe, whose endless encouragement has been invaluable from the first draft to accompanying me on half these rides... on a gravel bike!

Front cover: Descending the bridleway that traverses the eastern face of Lonscale Fell (photo: Adam Walton)

Contents

Overview maps . . . . Inside front cover –1
Map key 6
Route summary table 8

Introduction 11

What is bikepacking? 12
Individual time trials 14
Choice of bike 15
When to go 16
Mountain weather 16
Getting there and around 16
Accommodation 17
Fuel strategies 19
Kit 21
Cash and money 23
Navigation 23
Rights of way 24
The National Cycle Network 24
Safety and emergencies 24
Using this guide 25

The rides 29

Route 1	The Lakeland 200 30
Route 2	Furness Forests 54
Route 3	The Old Man of Coniston and the Irish Sea 68
Route 4	Way Out in the Western Fells 80
Route 5	Helvellyn and Back 94
Route 6	Dalston/Skiddaw Mega Pretzel 108
Route 7	Penrith/High Street Circuit 122
Route 8	Nine Lakes 134

Appendix A Lake District campsites and hostels 156
Appendix B Lake District bike shops 167
Appendix C Kit list 169

Symbols used on route maps

SCALE: 1:100,000

Contour lines are drawn at 50m intervals and labelled at 100m intervals. Route maps are drawn at 1:100,000 (1cm = 1km)

GPX files for all routes can be downloaded free at www.cicerone.co.uk/1117/GPX.

Features on the overview map

— County/Unitary boundary

Urban area

National Park
eg **THE LAKE DISTRICT**

Area of Outstanding Natural Beauty eg *Solway Coast*

An easy start back to Skiddaw from Peter House Farm (Route 6)

Bikepacking in the Lake District

Route summary table

Route		Start/Finish	Total distance	Off-road distance
1	The Lakeland 200	Barley Bridge, Staveley	209.6km/130 miles	149km
2	Furness Forests	Oxenholme Railway Station	103.3km/64 miles	44.4km
3	The Old Man of Coniston and the Irish Sea	Silecroft Railway Station/ Foxfield Railway Station	75.2km/46½ miles	31km
4	Way Out in the Western Fells	Whitehaven Railway Station	115.5km/72 miles	27km
5	Helvellyn and Back	Windermere Railway Station	95.9km/59½ miles	48km
6	Dalston/Skiddaw Mega Pretzel	Dalston Railway Station	123.5km/76½ miles	51km
7	Penrith/High Street Circuit	Penrith Railway Station	84km/52 miles	46km
8	Nine Lakes	Windermere Railway Station	254.7km/158¼ miles	53km

Route summary table

% off-road	Ascent/descent	Grade	Time	Way type (single-track, track, road)	Bike choice	Page
72%	6170m	◆/Very hard	3–5 days	32%, 40%, 28%	MTB	30
41%	1890m	●/Moderate	2–3 days	10%, 31%, 59%	Gravel/MTB	54
40%	2210m	◆/Hard	2–3 days	31%, 9%, 60%	Gravel/MTB	68
23%	2170m	▲/Moderate	2–3 days	9%, 14%, 77%	Gravel/MTB	80
50%	2440m	◆/Hard	2–3 days	14%, 36%, 50%	MTB	94
40%	2040m	●/Hard	2–3 days	14%, 26%, 60%	Gravel/MTB	108
55%	2060m	●/Hard	2–3 days	21%, 34%, 45%	Gravel/MTB	122
22%	4590m	◆/Very hard	3–5 days	11%, 10%, 79%	Gravel/MTB	134

The heart of the Skiddaw Massif (Route 6)

Looking north to Binsey from Dash Falls (Route 6)

Introduction

Looking down to Loweswater (Route 4)

The Lake District is an exceptional location for bikepacking. No other location has the density of first-class off-road riding within such a varied and wild landscape. Its 16 lakes are flanked by dozens of fells (an Old Norse term which means mountains and hills), and over 3000km of rights of way criss-cross its 912 square miles. It's a varied landscape with almost 10,000 hectares of managed plantation and one-third more of deciduous woodland. Beyond the Victoriana of Beatrix Potter and Wordsworth that is the signature style of some of the busy towns, the area has been a working agricultural landscape for millennia. The many pack-roads pre-date the 19th-century tourist boom. Its grazing land and forestry are actively managed.

To help the inquisitive adventurer, Alfred Wainwright partitioned Lakeland into seven areas: the Western Fells, the North Western Fells, the Northern Fells, the Southern Fells, the Central Fells, the Far Eastern Fells, and the Eastern Fells. This ambitious guide will introduce the rider to all of these, with two of the routes featuring all seven. When you have completed these routes you will have

Bikepacking in the Lake District

had an almost unique exposure to the Lake District, having explored every type of landscape and habitat it has to offer. From nights in the woods with just owls for company to welcoming inns with first-class food and beer and great company, the Lake District has something for every explorer.

What is bikepacking?

Bikepacking, like backpacking, involves heading off on a journey that's going to take you more than one day to complete. For this reason, you're going to need to take a few things with you to improve your comfort when you are not riding your bike (see Appendix C). At the least, you will need a tent (or bivvy bag) and sleeping bag if you are camping, and some food and possibly a way of preparing it.

Bikepacking differs from classic cycle touring principally in respect to the terrain you will be covering and the bike you will be riding. Instead of a paved road, you are heading out onto bridle paths, byways, green lanes, forestry tracks and long-abandoned rights of way. That's not to say there won't be times when taking the road is the best choice or when a B&B or YHA is a sensible option, but for the most part bikepacking can be defined as an off-road camping trip taken on a bike.

It also differs from classical mountain biking. The reader shouldn't expect these pages to be filled with endless high-octane, single-track

The view back to the Irish Sea (Route 4)

A tough hike-a-bike...but worth it (Route 5)

descents (although there are plenty of these). Bikepacking is more a form of exploration. Becoming fully immersed in the glacial geology, stone-walled farmland and wilderness is a pilgrimage in itself. As Nan Shepherd, the pioneering Scottish poet and writer, would say: the experience is about better knowing 'the total mountain'. Some of these routes are challenging but each provides the opportunity to embark on an awe-inspiring odyssey that will stay with you for a long time to come.

Hike-a-bike

Each of these rides contains some sections where the terrain will force the rider to get off and push their bike. This is tiring and can be a bit of a drag...literally. If it's extremely steep, you can brake and then use the bike's rigid position to pull your body forward. It's also helpful to keep the weight down: take as little equipment as possible. Carbon bike frames are lighter than steel.

It's worth remembering that your bike enables you to travel great distances that would be impossible by foot in the same timeframe, enabling you to reach these passes without a car. It acts as your packhorse, carrying the weight of your kit that would otherwise be on your back and ankles. It can also stabilise you when traversing difficult terrain on both the ascent and the descent. And, finally, it allows you to make a swift descent to your camp or the train on the other side.

Individual time trials

The Lakeland 200 is a recognised Individual Time Trial (ITT). These types of route have been devised to test the rider, and have gained popularity as 'classics'. They exist in the popular imagination and are occasionally the focus of events. More are collected here: www.selfsupporteduk.net. They are challenging enough to provide something for even the most seasoned of riders.

It hasn't escaped our notice that even by describing the Lakeland 200 in a guide we are providing some sort of support. However, reading about the route in advance or while you are on route is not against the rules and if this guide encourages more riders to take on these challenges in this style then this has to be a positive. The website lists fastest times, distances, start points and ascents in metres. Crucially, the philosophy centres around self-reliance, your fitness, and your previous experience of travelling fast and light and sustaining yourself for days in the wild landscape.

However, while the Lakeland 200 is a stone-cold classic and we encourage you to dig deep and take it on, that's not the exclusive focus of this guide. Only a small number of riders are going to be able to complete that route over a weekend, and it will be a brutal and sleepless experience for them. The other routes in this guide are designed to be ridden over 2–3 days and are achievable, accessible and less demanding. You can jump on a train after work on a Friday and bivvy in the national park that night before

Individual time trial rules

There are rules that must be followed when riding these routes as Individual Time Trials (taken verbatim from the website):

- Complete the entire route, under your own power – no drafting
- Be completely self-supported throughout the ride – absolutely no support crews, absolutely no gear sharing
- Only use commercial services that are available to all challengers – no private resupply, no private lodging
- If you have to leave the route, you must rejoin it at exactly the same spot
- No caches of any kind
- No pre-arranged support, which means before you begin your ride – e.g. booking a B&B, arranging to meet a vehicle
- No travel by any motorised means during your ride – by all means do so if necessary, but understand if you do your attempt is over.

Every shade of green – the view along Glenderaterra Beck (Route 6)

setting off on an incredible adventure when the sun comes up the next morning. I've done that many times and can't recommend it enough!

We have provided alternative schedules that vary in length from 2–5 days depending on how far you intend to travel and at what level of intensity of speed. A list of campsites is included in Appendix A. There are many ways to approach these rides and these landscapes. The important thing is to know your limitations, and when, or if, you intend to push them on a particular ride.

Choice of bike

Take the right bike for the terrain. The Lakeland 200 is certainly a MTB route and as the Lakes contain the highest peaks in England, unsurprisingly the majority of the bridleways are steep and rocky. There are paved sections and some of the farm and forestry tracks are excellent fun on a gravel bike; in fact, most of the routes have been ridden on a gravel bike, but in truth there is not much gravel riding in the Lakes. Many routes are characterised by difficult hike-a-bike ascents and treacherous rocky descents that are tough going on a gravel bike. Often a full suspension bike would be quite at home here.

Whatever bike you take, make sure it's been serviced recently and that you have the tools and knowledge to make basic repairs. Make sure you take enough inner tubes, lights and any other replacement parts you might need. Bike shops in the area are listed in Appendix B at the back of the guide.

When to go

This depends on the experience you are looking for. In the summer months and school holidays the Lakeland infrastructure can be tested to breaking point and campsites need to be booked in advance. Wild camping is less straightforward during peak times when every inch of the landscape is being enjoyed to the full. Spring and autumn are good options. You will avoid the extremes of both the weather and the crowds. The colours of the trees are exceptional in autumn, and in spring the verdant greens and brightly coloured flowers will cheer you up on the steepest of climbs.

Winter also has its own unique appeal: the drama of the landscape and the opportunity to experience the exclusive wilderness of the Lakes in winter. Avoid these routes in harsh winter conditions such as ice and snow. However, in mild winters the lower-level routes such as Furness Forests and Way Out in the Western Fells should be achievable. Fewer people makes the riding less hazardous but the trade-off may well be mud and less daylight. Planning needs to be tighter and on the longer rides, you may well need more days than you had planned for. Your tent should be three-season or four-season and your sleeping bag's comfort temperature should go down to 0°C. Keep in mind the notes below regarding emergency situations.

Mountain weather

Weather is unpredictable in the mountains and can change quickly. It's not advisable to take on high off-road passes if the weather is unsettled or if it's late in the day. It's useful to obtain a summary from the Mountain Weather Information Service (MWIS) when planning your ride: www.mwis.org.uk. The Met Office weather phone app or the Dark Skies phone app are also accurate and are more localised than other apps.

Getting there and around

The Lake District is situated in the north west of England, bordered on the east by Northumberland, Durham and North Yorkshire, and to the west by the Irish Sea. The routes in this guide have been designed to start and end at one of the many railway stations dotted around the edges of the national park. This decision was made for three reasons: firstly, train travel is more sustainable than travel by car; secondly, the rider will be introduced to the more remote and unspoilt Lakeland towns; and thirdly, it would be difficult to reach some of these areas by car, either because of their remoteness or because of their popularity!

If you are planning a journey by train it's essential to book a space for

Accommodation

your bike on the train in advance to avoid disappointment. Messaging Avanti West Coast on Facebook Messenger is the fastest way to get a response. Once you have a bike reservation always print out two copies of it, one for you and one to attach to your bike.

If you are planning to drive to the start of a circular route you can often park on a suburban street. Be considerate and avoid blocking people's drives. Be wary of local parking restrictions – you may be away from your car for a week if you are doing the Lakeland 200! Failing that, a long-stay car park might be your cheapest option. If starting in Carlisle, Penrith or Kendal, a Premier Inn is a good place to bookend your trip as they let you keep your vehicle in their car park for the nights you are away.

Accommodation

There are different ways to approach this. If you are following a strict Individual Time Trial riding style then you may be wild camping for the

Time for a snack at Brownhowe Bottom (Route 7)

Stones make good anchors when the soil is shallow (wild camp on Route 1)

whole trip. However, we would certainly not be as prescriptive as that. The main goal is to get out there and ride these routes, either on your own or ideally with others.

The Lake District offers a range of accommodation: campsites, shepherds' huts, glamping pods, hostels, camping barns and B&Bs. Where you choose to stay will be influenced by a number of factors, including the weather, how much experience you and the rest of your party have, your budget, and your need for flexibility. If the weather forecast is poor you can choose to either delay your trip, book some suitable accommodation in advance or take the requisite kit. However, mixing up your accommodation styles is a great alternative to rigidly following one approach. Perhaps it's going to be dry on the first night, rain on the second and then clear up for the rest of the ride? In that case you might decide to wild camp the first night, book into a B&B for the second night and use a campsite for the third evening. Or if you have three dry days followed by a wet day, you could camp for three nights and book into a hotel on the fourth to make use of their drying room for your wet gear and enjoy a hot meal instead of camp food.

Wild camping

This is defined as camping anywhere that isn't a licensed campsite. Although technically illegal in much of England, it is widely tolerated providing you adhere to the following rules and guidelines:

1. Camp high and away from settlements. Where possible head uphill, away from paths and buildings.
2. Respect the privacy of others.
3. Do not interfere with livestock.
4. Camp late and leave early. As the day's ride comes to an end, begin keeping your eye out for good spots so that you can identify a suitable camp spot before running out of light. In the morning, pack up your tent or bivvy before breakfast and get back on the road straight afterwards.
5. Only wild camp solo or in small groups to avoid disturbing the environment and your neighbours.
6. Bury human waste at least 10 inches deep with your shovel. Do not pollute any water courses. Take toilet paper and wipes home.
7. Leave no trace. Take all litter home.
8. Do not light an open fire.

Wild camping in the Lake District
The national park can be very busy in summer come rain or shine. It is also relatively populated in some areas with many people depending on the land for their livelihoods or their leisure. When you intend to wild camp, plan your ride so that you will be in a remote location as the day ends. It's unlikely that you will have any issues on Walna Scar or Scarth Gap, but in more densely populated places around Ambleside, Keswick and Coniston you will be competing for space or surrounded by exclusive properties. One good strategy that can be relied on is to study the map looking for bridleways that lead onto common land/access land (identified on OS Explorer® maps) near where you expect to be finishing that day. Often following these can lead you to good locations for a night's kip.

Fuel strategies

Riding a bike is a physically demanding activity, riding a bike for days over mountains even more so. You need to ask yourself a few questions about the ride you are about to do. Firstly, how self-supported will you and the rest of your party be? All riders need to be on a similar page regarding food, or at the least to have acknowledged before starting out that your expectations differ and that everyone is supportive of enabling these different choices. However, sometimes there may not be a choice to be had.

Bringing your own food
As with everything else, weight and packability is key here. We would advise against attempting a fried breakfast or making a stew from scratch. Avoid 'cooking' anything if you can. Instead consider doing some combination of the following: eat things that don't need to be warmed like oatcakes, cheese, chorizo and fruit. Reheat pre-made food such

Bikepacking in the Lake District

as boil-in-the-bag camping meals, beans or other canned meals, or use dehydrated food which you can reconstitute with boiling water. Rehydration has some advantages here because dehydrated food is very light to carry, (almost) never goes off and all it requires is boiling water, some patience (30min wait to rehydrate a portion of vegetable curry) and something to insulate the food while it rehydrates (a sleeping bag or down jacket is perfect). You can make it in advance yourself (my preferred approach) or buy from specialists.

Rely on local infrastructure

A good pub lunch is a treat you can hopefully squeeze in. Dropping into a Co-op and picking up a few provisions towards the end of a day's riding can sometimes be planned to avoid carrying weighty items (a micro-rucksack comes in handy here). There is also scope for arriving at a pub and getting dinner at the end of the day and then heading off to bivvy under the stars, although it's always worth checking what time they stop taking orders for food. There are some cracking pubs in the Lake District that should be visited if the opportunity presents.

Taking a breather halfway over Gale Fell (Route 4)

Coffee on its way

Hybrid model
You can mix things up. Perhaps bring your own breakfast in the form of overnight oats with dried fruit, or granola with milk powder, or apple juice in a silicone pouch. You could also bring a few portions of dehydrated food as backup but take advantage of local refreshment options as you pass them.

Snacks
Dried fruit, nuts, cereal bars and protein bars are all great snacking options. These are all commercially available or can be made in advance.

Hydration
The importance of keeping hydrated cannot be understated. Take every opportunity to refill your water bottles. There is no need to carry large quantities of water with you as there are countless streams you can refill from. You can filter the water; Sawyer is a brand to look out for (the Sawyer Micro is Nicky's favourite, chosen over the Mini for its flow rate). Consider adding electrolyte powder to improve hydration but remember to keep some of your water free from electrolytes if you are planning to use it to make coffee or hydrate food with! Plan before setting out and give yourself options.

Kit
There are many factors that influence what you will need to take with you, not least what the weather is going to be doing, where you plan to sleep and what you are doing for food.

Starting the exceptional descent into Mickleden (Route 5)

Fast and light

The bulk of the riding in these routes is off-road and much of it hilly. Whatever you take with you, you will be hauling it up bridleways and dragging it over hills. When deciding what to take, your decision should be influenced by the conditions you expect to face after reviewing the weather forecast for the days you intend to be out and then allowing a sensible margin for error.

You should aspire to take the lightest kit that will get the job done. For example, don't take your lightest summer sleeping bag if the overnight temperature is going to dip to −1. Think twice about a tarp set up if there is heavy rain expected on the morning of day three. Beyond these practical considerations, the lighter your load is, the more comfortable you will be. Scrutinise each item you intend to take and ask yourself if it is essential. If possible a piece of kit should be tried and tested and, ideally, perform more than one function.

A word on base layer fabrics: if you are planning multiple nights camping outside of the summer months, merino wool is a good choice for base layers as it is very warm, has great wicking properties and is relatively odourless. For shorter summer rides, you might prefer synthetic mesh materials for wicking and comfort.

See Appendix C for a kit list.

Cash and money

In the larger towns such as Ambleside, Coniston, Windermere, Whitehaven and Keswick there is no shortage of cash machines. Many of the pubs and shops you will visit will also accept card payments; however, this cannot be guaranteed. In some villages the tea room or campsite will be 'cash only' so make sure you have a few notes kept in reserve for such occasions.

Navigation

We provide GPX of each of the routes in this book. These can be loaded onto a bar-mounted cycling computer or mobile phone.

There are many great apps out there to help you navigate the trail. Many of these products have desktop counterparts that allow you to import the GPX files and view them in the context of the surrounding countryside; it's worth doing this before you set out. These tools can also be used to help you plan and design your own routes. They often contain routes and rides submitted by their online communities which can be a good source of inspiration.

Remember to set your phone to airplane mode to save battery – GPS will still work. Also, while still on Wi-Fi, download the maps to your phone for later offline use.

Paper maps come into their own

Bikepacking in the Lake District

However, whether you use a phone or bike computer, it's always best to avoid relying exclusively on one navigation aid. GPS head units can fail, especially when their lithium batteries get cold (if this happens, put them in a pocket close to your skin to keep them warm). Mobile phones can run out of battery. Make sure you have at least one battery power bank. Take a physical map and compass and know how to use them.

Rights of way

Riders are permitted to use bridleways, cycleways, green lanes and permissive bridleways. You are not permitted to ride on footpaths.

The National Cycle Network

This network of routes, managed by Sustrans UK, is a wonderful resource. The routes in this guide often take advantage of these when linking up sections of off-road cycling. They can be guaranteed to be relatively quiet and are often picturesque.

Safety and emergencies

Ensure you have a mobile phone as well as (multiple) ways of keeping it charged. In the event of serious injury call 999 and request the required service: ambulance if you are on the road; police and then mountain rescue if you are off the road. Give them your location, ideally by grid reference, and your phone number.

The open fell of Mosedale Moss (Route 6)

What Three Words (W3W) is used by many emergency services to aid rescue. In mountainous situations where there is no guarantee of phone signal a satellite phone such as the Garmin inReach Mini can be used. Take time to become familiar with this before setting out. It is also worth registering your phone with the emergency SMS service. This allows anyone who is deaf, hard of hearing or speech impaired to text the emergency services, and can also be used by anyone when signal does not allow for a phone call.

Always pack a spare head torch, a space blanket, a whistle and emergency food. Make sure your sleeping bag is suitable for the overnight temperatures. Never be completely reliant on a single mobile phone; it can easily become a point of failure. Ensure there are multiple devices in your group, that maps are downloaded, that you keep a power pack charged and handy, and consider carrying a paper map and compass.

Within Cumbria there are four hospitals providing A&E services:

- Barrow,
  Dalton Ln,
  Barrow-in-Furness, LA14 4LF
- Carlisle,
  Newton Rd, Carlisle, CA2 7HY
- Kendal,
  Burton Rd, Kendal, LA9 7RG
- Whitehaven,
  30 Homewood Hill,
  Whitehaven, CA28 8JY

Using this guide

The main factors influencing route choice are time, difficulty, expected weather and conditions, and ease of accessing the start point. All these rides start and end at or near railway stations so depending on where you are coming from, journey time to the start will influence your choice of route. With the exception of the Lakeland 200 and the Nine Lakes, these rides are designed to be ridden over two or three days.

None of these routes should be considered suitable for novice riders. While some are easier than others, each is challenging and will involve some hike-a-bike. Lakeland is extremely hilly and these routes, two of which are over 200km, seek out pack-roads, green lanes and bridleways with most of the routes taking on one or two off-road passes in each day's riding.

Each route has the following components: Information Box, Introduction, Overview, Summary Table, Schedules, Alternative Start/Finish, Map, Route Profile and Turn-by-Turn Directions.

The Route Summary Table at the beginning of the book or the route Information Box at the beginning of the route is the first place to look when choosing a route. They include crucial information: start/finish location, length, grade (based on the hardest stage), percentage of off-road, and bike choice. The Summary

Table in the route then provides the same information for each numbered stage within the route. These stages can be understood as logical blocks within a route, although are not necessarily equal in length – they correlate more closely to terrain or options for refuelling or rest. The Introduction points out the merits and features of the route while the Overview is a high-level description of the route. The elevation profile is useful for strategising where you can refuel and camp. In most cases, we have provided a few suggestions for alternative starts and finishes for the route. For obvious reasons, if you choose to take advantage of these this will affect the stage order; only choose these if you are comfortable with picking up the route on your GPS and don't have an issue jumping backwards or forwards in the directions.

The main component is the Turn-by-Turn Directions, which you can follow alongside the inline map if you need to rely on the guide rather than the GPX on a device. We do suggest that you read through these instructions before making your final choice of route (rather than in the rain on a windy bluff). Often the routes come with shortcuts or extensions and it's helpful to assess the relative merits of these before heading out on the ride. A river crossing may only be recommended in summer months, or a route off a mountain may be advisable if time is short or the weather takes a turn. Consider timings, difficulty, and expected weather conditions. Forewarned is forearmed. Use the Schedules table to determine a suitable schedule. This will be influenced by a few factors, not least the weather, the hours of riding in a day you can commit to and the hours of daylight. You may only have two days to spare or maybe you want to take it easier and take a long weekend over it.

The routes are designed to position the rider in a location where they can find good accommodation and food options at the end of the day. Depending on your style (and the weather!) you can book in advance or turn up and review your choices, but either way it pays to scope out your options and have a plan before you head out. Use the route profile provided to help to anticipate the road ahead. You may want to refuel before taking on a climb or plan to camp after a descent. The profile also includes icons that inform the rider of the amenities available at a given location.

Direction arrows are used to indicate ← (left), → (right) and ↑ (straight ahead).

Overall route grades

While this guide relies on the classic MTB grading system to suggest the technical difficulty of each section within a route (see below), the routes as a whole have been given both a technical MTB grade (the grade of the hardest stage of that route) and an overall grade that takes the route's

The northern approach to Skiddaw House (Route 6)

other qualities into account. All the rides present challenges, but some are more challenging than others. In some cases, such as the Nine Lakes (Route 8), this is given a 'very hard' grade owing to its length and the inclusion of a couple of high off-road passes; in the case of Lakeland 200 (Route 1), the 'very hard' grade is given for its relentless severity as well as distance. Two of the rides are 'moderate'; the other four are 'hard'.

MTB grades

Road stages have not been graded. Any hard road sections can be identified through warnings in the guide and arrows on the map.

The grades for off-road sections are adapted from www.britishcycling.org.uk:

- **Green/Easy:** No special cycling skills, even ground, un-challenging, shallow climbs, suitable for all riders.

- **Blue/Moderate:** Mountain bikers with basic off-road riding skills. Minor obstacles, moderate gradients with occasional steep sections. Descents can be steep and include some semi-technical features.

- **Red/Difficult:** Proficient mountain bikers with good off-road riding skills. Steeper and tougher, mostly single-track with technical sections. Expect variable surface types. A wide range of climbs and descents of a challenging nature. Expect boardwalks, large rocks, medium steps, drop-offs, cambers and water crossings. Higher level of fitness and stamina.

- ◆ **Black/Severe:** Expert mountain bike users, used to physically demanding routes. As 'Red' but with an expectation of greater challenge and continuous difficulty. Can include any useable trail surface and may include exposed open hill sections. Expect large, committing and unavoidable technical features. Sections will be challenging and variable. May also have 'downhill' style sections. Suitable for very active people used to prolonged effort.

GPX tracks

GPX tracks for the routes in this guidebook are available to download free at www.cicerone.co.uk/1117/GPX. If you have not bought the book through the Cicerone website, or have bought the book without opening an account, please register your purchase in your Cicerone library to access GPX and update information.

A GPS device is an excellent aid to navigation, but you should also carry a map and compass and know how to use them. GPX files are provided in good faith, but in view of the profusion of formats and devices, neither the author nor the publisher accepts responsibility for their use. We provide files in a single standard GPX format that works on most devices and systems, but you may need to convert files to your preferred format using a GPX converter such as gpsvisualizer.com or one of the many other apps and online converters available.

The rides

Beginning a tricky single-track descent (Route 2)

1

72% off road

Route 1
The Lakeland 200

Start/finish	Barley Bridge, north side of Staveley (grid ref SD 46989 98701)
Total distance	209.6km (130 miles)
Off-road distance	149km
Percentage off-road	72%
Total ascent/descent	6170m
Grade	Very hard ◆
Time	3–5 days
Terrain	Single-track 32%, track 40%, road 28%
Bike choice	MTB

Introduction

The drama of the Cumbrian Mountains comes from the abrupt way they rise from their surroundings; here England's deepest lake, Wast Water, is flanked by its highest peak, Scafell Pike.

The Lakeland 200 was devised by Alan Goldsmith as an Individual Time Trial (ITT – see Introduction) and the tour circumnavigates the Lake District. The climbs are often steep and unpaved but always rewarding. The descents are often single-track and technical. Every kilometre is hard-won with the route containing its fair share of hike-a-bike sections, windswept escarpments, forestry single-track and open fell. Fortunately, these challenges are punctuated by welcoming towns accustomed to weary riders in search of refreshments.

We provide schedules for two, three, four or five days.

Little Gatesgarthdale

Overview

Begin in Staveley, accessible by train via Oxenholme Lake District Rail Station. The first 55km is the warm-up. Head north up Kentmere from Staveley then down into Troutbeck before heading around Wansfell into Ambleside. Traverse around Loughrigg Fell to Elterwater before reaching Langdale, then continue through Grizedale Forest before dropping into Coniston. Now the climbing starts and the altitude triples to 640m over 5km, topping out on the shoulder of the Old Man of Coniston. A stunning descent is followed by a dogleg around Dunnerdale Fells leading to the hamlet of Seathwaite. After a short section of the Duddon Valley, a bridleway goes around Harter Fell and down to Jubilee Bridge at the foot of Hardknott Pass. Advance along the Esk Valley into Boot before heading over exposed fell towards Wast Water. The next challenge is the infamous Black Sail Pass closely followed by Scarth Gap before heading into Gatesgarth. Climb Honister Pass on road before descending on a spectacular single-track into Borrowdale. From there it's on to Keswick and Lonscale Fell beyond. After Threlkeld, cross the exposed northern shoulder of Matterdale. From here find a way east around to Pooley Bridge before continuing south again towards Martindale and over Bedafell Knott. The final challenge goes over High Street, a spectacular exposed ridge at 810m, before the route heads back to Staveley.

Summary table

Waypoint	Section	Distance (km)	Ascent (m)	Descent (m)
1	Staveley – Troutbeck	11	180	130
2	Troutbeck – Ambleside	5.2	120	210
3	Ambleside – Chapel Stile	9.1	230	200
4	Chapel Stile – Knipe Fold	9.1	220	170
5	Knipe Fold – Low Wray	4.3	10	100
6	Low Wray – Grizedale	11.7	320	260
7	Grizedale – Coniston	7.7	160	230
8	Coniston – Disused quarry after Walna Scar Road	6.4	535	140
9	Disused quarry after Walna Scar Road – Seathwaite	10.1	150	470
10	Seathwaite – Jubilee Bridge	10.1	250	250
11	Jubilee Bridge – Boot	6.7	70	140
12	Boot – Wasdale Head	9	280	240
13	Wasdale Head – YHA Black Sail Hut	5.2	450	255
14	YHA Black Sail Hut – Gatesgarth	3.6	160	345
15	Gatesgarth – Honister Pass	4.5	250	60
16	Honister Pass – Grange	5	50	260
17	Grange – Keswick	8.4	175	180
18	Keswick – Threlkeld	11.9	360	280
19	Threlkeld – High Row	10.5	370	110
20	High Row – Pooley Bridge	12.9	140	410
21	Pooley Bridge – St Peter's Church, Martindale	9.4	260	170
22	St Peter's Church, Martindale – Hartsop	9.1	310	370
23	Hartsop – The Knott	3.9	550	0
24	The Knott – Limefitt Park	11.4	220	720
25	Limefitt Park – Staveley	13.4	350	470

Route 1 – The Lakeland 200

Surface	Grade	Description
mixture paved/unpaved	🟩	After a warm-up, head over fields before a sharp descent into Troutbeck
mixture paved/unpaved	🟩	A steep climb with some great views before dropping into Ambleside
mixture paved/unpaved	🔺	A picturesque section with some tricky wooded descents and difficult wayfinding
mixture paved/unpaved	🟩	Difficult wayfinding, take care
unpaved	🟩	Picturesque minor roads
unpaved	🔺	Rough track and wooded climbing
unpaved	🔺	Secluded forestry delivers you to historical Coniston where there is opportunity to refuel
unpaved	♦	A tough climb out of Coniston before the Walna Scar Road takes you over the shoulder of the Old Man of Coniston
unpaved	🔴	Great views but indistinct paths and tricky wayfinding before a fast single-track descent into Seathwaite
mixture paved/unpaved	🔺	A welcome road section leads to a tough bridleway around lonely Harter Fell
unpaved	🟩	Easy rolling through the Esk Valley to refreshments in Boot
unpaved	🔺	Tough hike-a-bike onto exposed fell before single-track descent into Wasdale
unpaved	♦	Two–three hours of hike-a-bike leads you to secluded Ennerdale
unpaved	♦	Easier than the previous section but still tough. Outstanding views of the Buttermere Fells
paved	🟩	Hard road climbing to an exposed pass
unpaved	🔴	Beautiful descent into Borrowdale
mixture paved/unpaved	🔺	A few hard climbs before joining a purpose-built MTB single-track into Keswick
unpaved	🔺	A long climb followed by a flat, exposed section providing stunning views
unpaved	🔺	A linking road section before a slow climb out over exposed fell
paved	🟩	Easy but fiddly linking section
unpaved	🟩	A short climb followed by great single-track with stunning views
unpaved	🔴	Difficult wayfinding is followed by exhausting hike-a-bike over an exposed pass
unpaved	♦	Short road section followed by strenuous hike-a-bike
unpaved	🔴	Exposed ridgeway followed by a breathtaking single-track descent
unpaved	🔺	The home straight: a short climb and fiddly wayfinding

Schedules

km from Staveley
Total length of route 209.6km

Section	Location	km
	Staveley	0
Section 1		
	Troutbeck	10
Section 2	Ambleside	
Section 3		20
	Chapel Stile	
Section 4		30
	Knipe Fold	
Section 5	Low Wray	40
Section 6		
	Grizedale	50
Section 7		
	Coniston	60
Section 8	Disused quarry after Walna Scar Road	
Section 9		70
	Seathwaite	
Section 10		80
	Hardknott Pass	
Section 11		90
	Boot	
Section 12		
	Wasdale Head	100
Section 13	Black Sail YHA	
Section 14	Gatesgarth	110
Section 15	Honister Pass	
Section 16		
	Grange	120
Section 17		
	Keswick	130
Section 18		
	Threlkeld	140
Section 19		
	High Row	150
Section 20		
		160
	Pooley Bridge	
Section 21		170
	St Peter's Church Martindale	
Section 22		
Section 23	Hartsop	180
	The Knott	
Section 24		190
	Limefitt Park	200
Section 25		
	Staveley	210

2 DAYS (10hrs pd / Av 11 kph)	3 DAYS (8hrs pd / 8.5 kph)	4 DAYS (6hrs pd / 7 kph)	5 DAYS (5hrs pd / 6 kph)
Sections 1–13 Staveley to Black Sail Hut YHA *105.6km 2975m ascent*	**Sections 1–9** Staveley to Seathwaite *74.6km 1925m ascent*	**Sections 1–7** Staveley to Coniston *58.1km 1240m ascent*	**Sections 1–5** Staveley to Low Wray *38.7km 760m ascent*
			Sections 6–9 Low Wray to Seathwaite *35.9km 1165m ascent*
		Sections 8–12 Coniston to Wasdale Head *42.3km 1285m ascent*	
	Sections 10–19 Seathwaite to High Row *74.9km 2415m ascent*		**Sections 10–13** Seathwaite to Black Sail Hut YHA *31km 1050m ascent*
Sections 14–25 Black Sail Hut YHA to Staveley *104km 3195m ascent*		**Sections 13–19** Wasdale Head to High Row *49.1km 1815m ascent*	**Sections 14–20** Black Sail Hut YHA to Pooley Bridge *56.8km 1505m ascent*
	Sections 20–25 High Row to Staveley *60.1km 1830m ascent*	**Sections 20–25** High Row to Staveley *60.1km 1830m ascent*	**Sections 21–25** Pooley Bridge to Staveley *47.2km 1690m ascent*

Route 1 – The Lakeland 200

Alternative start/finish suggestions

The official start of the route is Staveley. This works well for people travelling from the south by car or train. If you are coming from the north of the country by car, Pooley Bridge or Keswick would make a good place to start. If you wish to journey in from the west, consider taking the Ravenglass Railway to Dalegarth (requires booking if transporting a bike).

Directions

1 ■ Follow Brow Foot Lane, the road on the west side of the river, up Kentmere Valley until you reach a T-junction at the top of the hill. Turn → onto a bridleway. Follow this as it bears ←. After 1.5km turn →. Continue past High Borrans Centre on Borrans Lane for 2km until you reach a road. Turn → onto Moorhowe Road and progress for 2km before taking a → onto Longmire Road bridleway and following ↑ for 1.5km until you meet a fork. Take a sharp ←. Follow a track that becomes a set of cobblestone steps. At the junction turn → to **Troutbeck**.

2 ■ Continue over a bridge. Turn ← onto a bridleway after the church. On reaching the road take a ←. After 125 metres turn → onto Robin Lane and follow this steep bridleway around the southern shoulder of **Wansfell**. At 1.25km take the ← fork. Progress downhill for 1km. Take a → at the junction. Follow the bridleway for 2km before taking a → onto the main road into **Ambleside**.

> **Ambleside** is one of three decent-sized towns on the route, Coniston and Keswick being the other two. It's an opportunity to grab outstanding supplies or visit a bike shop. There are accommodation options in Appendix A.

3 ▲ Follow Lake Rd briefly before turning ← on Wansfell Road, signposted Keswick/Coniston/Hawkshead. At the T-junction turn ←. Bear ← on Borrans Road one-way system for 300 metres before turning →, then turn ← over Rothay Bridge before turning → onto Under Loughrigg Road. After 800 metres turn ← onto a bridleway. Climb out onto the southern shoulder of **Loughrigg Fell**. Follow a track over open land with views of Lake Windermere. After 3km a sharp → takes you past Loughrigg Tarn. Follow the track until you rejoin the road and advance ↑ for 600 metres before taking a sharp ←. Maintain your direction until **Chapel Stile**. Turn ← before the church. Head downhill through the town and turn ← at the junction. Continue for 200 metres.

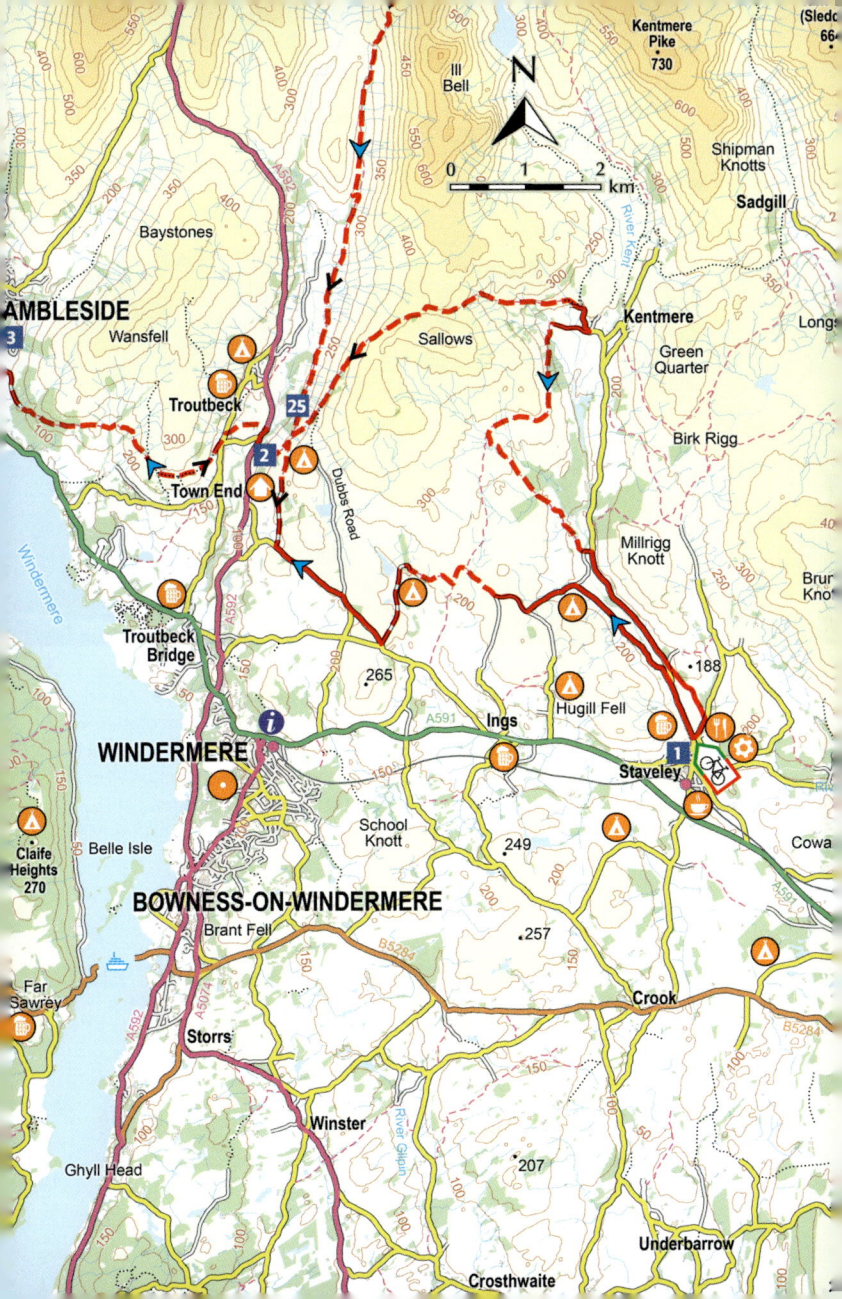

Loughrigg Tarn, north of Skelwith Bridge

4 ■ Cross the road before heading over a footbridge and turning →. Ascend ↑ through a slate works for 700 metres. Turn → and then immediately ← into Sawrey's Wood. After 550 metres take the → fork and follow the track downhill for 1km. Descend on the bridleway, bearing → at the junction where the route meets the off-road NCN 37. After 200 metres, join the road at Dale End. After a further 200 metres turn ←, signed Little Langdale. After 100

Route 1 – The Lakeland 200

metres turn ➔ and continue on the NCN 37. Keep following the road until the ford over Brathay River. After the bridge fork ➔ onto the NCN 637. At the next junction take the ⬅ fork and cross Pierce How Beck. Follow the track to Hodge Close. Bear ⬅, then cross NCN 637 and immediately turn ➔ heading east to High Oxen Fell. Ignoring the fork to the left, continue for 300 metres until you reach the A593. Here you can head straight down the A593 into Coniston as a shortcut. Cross the road and join the Cumbria Way. Continue on the Cumbria Way for 2.5km until you reach **Knipe Fold**.

5 ■ At the T-junction turn ⬅ and then quickly fork ➔ out of the hamlet. After 1.25km turn ⬅ at the junction with the B5286. Turn R here for the shortcut road to Coniston, Hawkshead and campsites at Hawkshead Hall and The Croft. Take the road ⬆ through **Outgate** before forking ➔ onto a bridleway. When you meet the road turn ➔ towards High Wray. For the campsite turn L into Low Wray. Climb ⬆ to **High Wray**.

6 ▲ After the junction take the bridleway on the left. After 450 metres turn ➔ and follow the track round to the ⬅ for 800 metres before forking ➔. Continue ⬆ for 1km before turning ➔ at the intersection of two tracks. Head ⬆. The track meets a road; continue on this until you arrive at the village of **Near Sawrey**. Turn ➔ then, after 100 metres, turn ⬅. Descend for 100 metres before forking ⬅ at the T-junction. Follow the road ⬆ for 1km over Ees Bridge. At the junction turn ➔ and advance for 700 metres before turning ⬅. Ascend for 175 metres before turning ➔ onto a bridleway. Progress ⬆ for 1.5km before turning ➔ at the next T-junction, then descend until you reach the hamlet of **Grizedale**. If you are looking to camp, descend L on the road towards Satterthwaite and you will reach Grizedale Campsite 500 metres beyond the village.

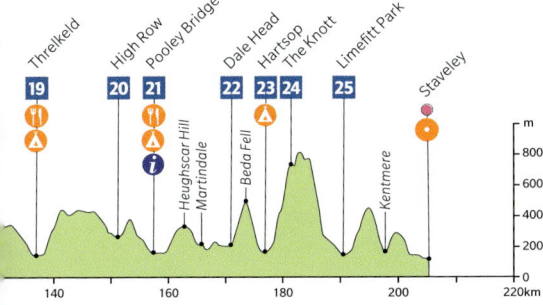

Route 1 – The Lakeland 200

7 ▲ Turn ← and then quickly turn → onto a track keeping the buildings on your right. Head towards the forest for 250 metres. Fork ← on a bridleway and after 50 metres take the → fork into Grizedale Forest. After 400 metres, turn → and then continue for 1.75km before taking a bridleway on the left. After 1km the track meets a road at Lawson Park. Head past Black Beck Cottage, then turn → and descend for 2km, with **Coniston Water** on your left beyond the trees, until the junction. Take the signs for Coniston and head round the northern end of Coniston Water and into **Coniston**.

> There are B&B options and two YHAs in **Coniston**, as well as chip shops and pubs offering standard fare. The Sun Hotel is an imposing sight as you climb through the town. This is the last built-up area before you take on some of the hardest parts of this route so consider stocking up or resting if necessary. Everything prior to this has been a warm-up; the next section is tough.

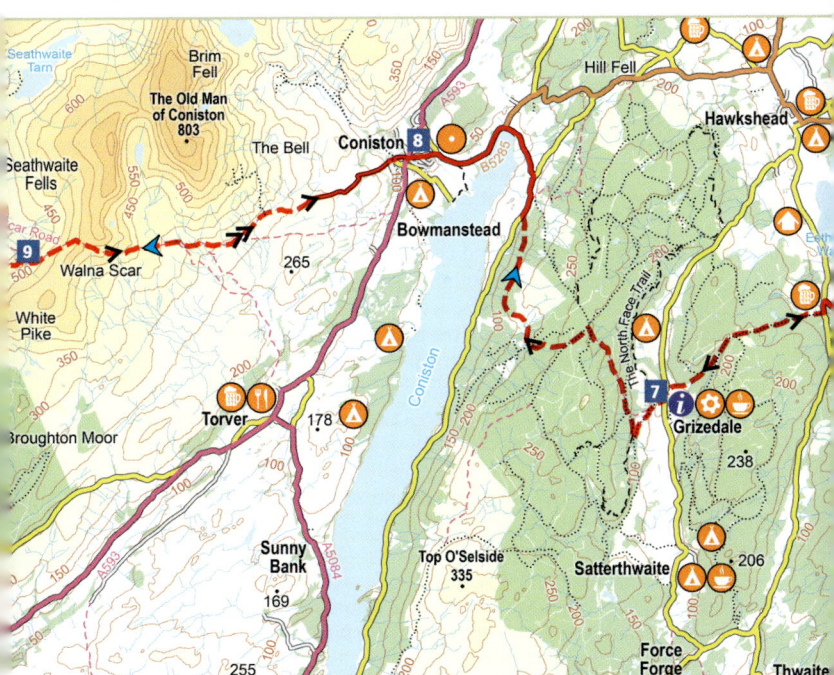

Bikepacking in the Lake District

8 ◆ Climb through Coniston. Take a → after The Sun Hotel. The following climb is a brutal 1:4. After this, enter Fell Gate car park. Head through the car park and join a road. Ascend to the pass on **Walna Scar Road**. The track descends steeply to the →. Take the bridleway until you meet a gate. Follow the wall to your left. The path leads to a small slate quarry. This is a good place to camp/bivvy.

> The climb over the southern shoulder of the **Old Man of Coniston** (803m) on the unpaved Walna Scar Road is 5km and climbs 365m to 640m. If you are a strong climber two-thirds of this is rideable, but some sections are very steep and rocky as the route makes a series of switches as it snakes upwards. You will have to carry your bike here.
>
> You can descend on the Walna Scar Road to Seathwaite and skip the next section entirely if you arrive late in the day or don't want to camp here.

9 ● Beyond the quarry, follow an indistinct bridleway over open fell and streams for 1.5km before forking → onto a single-track hugging the shoulder of **Caw**. After 2km the bridleway turns sharply → by a smallholding close to the road. Follow the walled path for 400 metres. Turn ← and head south for 1.5km with Raven's Crag on your right. When the path splits, take the → fork and continue north for 1.25km. Here it splits into three. Take the → fork heading north on Park Head Road (path) and descend into **Seathwaite**.

10 ▲ After two gates, turn → and continue through Seathwaite. 600 metres after meeting the road at Seathwaite, Turner Hall Farm Campsite is on your R (phone ahead). 4km after joining the road, take a bridleway on the left and cross a bridge across Tarn Beck. The path meets a car-wide track. Turn ←. Pass The Birks on your left. Go through a gate and turn ← at the junction. Progress for 5.25km on a car-wide track towards Dunnerdale Forest and around the edge of **Harter Fell** which becomes a single-track that descends to Jubilee Bridge at the foot of Hardknott Pass.

11 ■ When you meet the road, turn ← and advance until Whahouse Bridge before taking a sharp ← onto a bridleway. Continue across a field with the river on your right. Cross a narrow footbridge. Ascend for 200 metres through the wood before turning →. Follow the bridleway along the valley through fields, past farms and over a footbridge before reaching Dalegarth Hall and **Dalegarth campsite**. Follow the road over a bridge before turning → down a track. After 500 metres turn ← and follow the path until the crossroads in the

Bridge on the edge of Burnmoor Tarn

hamlet of **Boot**. Cross the main road with Brook House Inn on your left and progress ↑ towards the Eskdale Mill. Dalegarth Train Station is 200 metres to your left. There are two great pubs here: Brook House Inn and Boot Inn.

12 ▲ Continue past the mill through a gate. The path climbs steeply. Shortly fork → keeping Whillan Beck below you. Hike-a-bike gives way to a rideable section of track. To your right is **Eskdale Fell**; in front of you, beyond Illgil Head, is Yewbarrow. It feels very wild and exposed here. After 4km cross a wide footbridge. Skirt → around Burnmoor Tarn. After a shallow climb the descent, with **Wast Water** on the left, takes you into Wasdale. There's a car park and toilets at Wasdale Head. After 1.5km, Wasdale Inn is a welcoming place to stop for refreshments and camping can be had at the campsite in **Wasdale Head**.

> **Stages 13 and 14** are very challenging. If it's late, it would not be advisable to go much further than Wasdale Head before setting up camp. You need a minimum of three hours of daylight to get over Black Sail Pass and Scarth Gap.

Route 1 – The Lakeland 200

The historic Black Sail Hut YHA

13 ◆ Behind and to the right of the Wasdale Inn, the bridleway follows the riverbank. After 300 metres, cross an old packhorse bridge. Continue 100 metres through a gate and bear ←. The track becomes a rocky path. Halfway up the climb, cross a stream. Push your bike until you reach the pass. Follow a steep path downhill to Ennerdale Fell and the **Black Sail Hut YHA**.

> **Black Sail Hut YHA** is a special spot. It's sheltered from the worst weather on either side but still at 300m. There are good wild camping options here, especially in the winter months when the YHA is closed (Oct–March).

14 ◆ With the YHA hut on your right, follow the bridleway. When you reach a gate the car-wide track continues, but take a sharp → up steep steps to Scarth Gap. Descend on a steep single-track. Before you reach the valley floor take the → fork at the intersection of two paths. Fleetwith Pike dominates the skyline to your right. Progress ↑ on a neat bridleway between fields to Gatesgarth.

15 ■ Ascend for 3.5km up a steep valley to Honister Pass. From the summit follow the road for 1km before turning ← onto a rocky track that runs parallel to the road.

Fast descent into Borrowdale

16 ● After 800 metres of car-wide track, take the narrow bridleway that begins abruptly on your left and carves its way into the lower slopes of High Scawdel. Descend into Borrowdale Valley on a well-defined single-track. Castle Crag dominates your view as you descend into wooded glades along a steep rocky car-wide track for 3km. Cross two footbridges that form part of the Cumbria Way. A quiet road takes you past Chapel House Farm Campsite on your left and into **Grange**.

17 ▲ At the T-junction turn ←. Continue for 1.25km before taking a bridleway on the left and climbing the steep slopes of Mansty Band. After 250 metres take the → fork. Follow single-track until it meets the road again. Immediately take a path on your left and follow another single-track with views of **Derwent Water** to your right. After rejoining the road and following it for 100 metres, take the →. For the next 3.5km follow signs for Keswick. Head over a footbridge crossing the River Derwent before taking a → at a T-junction and continuing towards the town on High Hill Road before turning ← onto Crosthwaite Road.

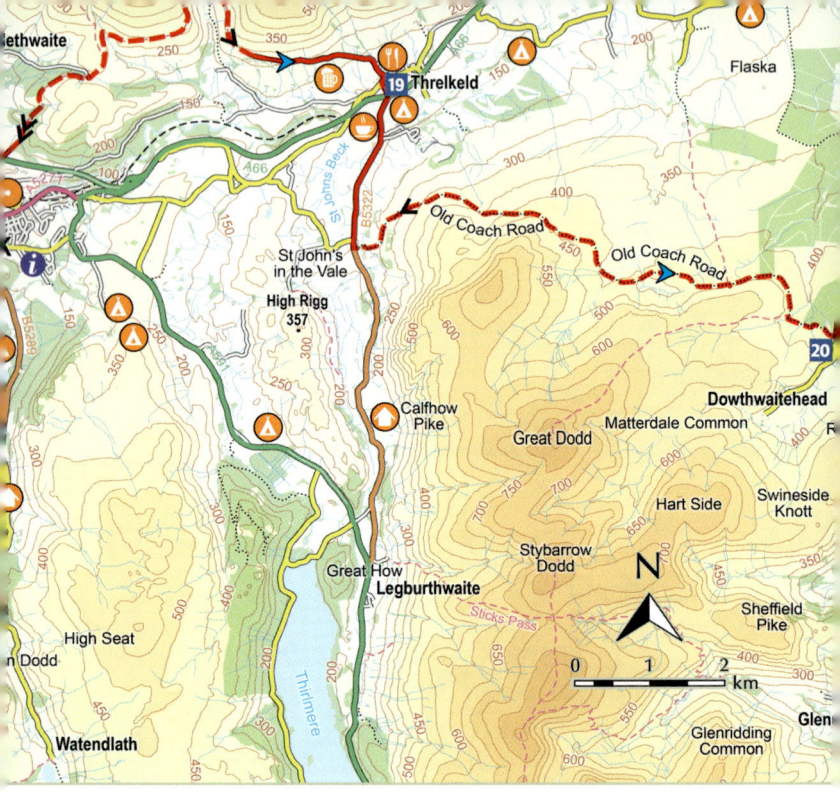

18 ▲ Take a → after the hospital onto Brundholme Road and then the first ← onto Spoony Green Lane which bridges the busy A66. Follow this track ↑ as it climbs the western slopes of Latrigg. When the track levels off, turn → at the gate. After 100 metres go through a second gate and turn ← onto the Cumbria Way. Follow the single-track as it hugs the steep slopes of **Lonscale Fell**. After 4km take a sharp → and cross Glenderaterra Beck and head in the opposite direction on the slopes of the adjacent Blease Fell. After 3.5km, pass Blencathra Outdoor Centre before joining Blease Road which delivers you to **Threlkeld**.

19 ▲ In the village centre turn →. After 100 metres turn ← onto Station Road. After 2.25km take a sharp ← onto a rough track signposted Matterdale. Follow the **Old Coach Road** snaking out over the exposed fell and topping out at 450m before meeting up with the road again at **High Row** 7.5km later.

Bikepacking in the Lake District

20 ■ At High Row turn ← at the crossroads. After 1.75km take a sharp → and continue for 2.75km through **Matterdale End** before turning → at a T-junction. At the village of **Cove** fork ←. In **Bennethead** take the → fork and advance ↑ until you meet the A592 and turn → to head along the edge of Ullswater into **Pooley Bridge**.

21 ■ Take the → over the bridge. After 275 metres turn → onto High Street. Continue to bear → until you fork → onto a car-wide track at the foot of **Heughscar Hill**. Climb to the brow of the hill. At the junction, signposted Howtown, head → over the fell. After 500 metres, reach Cock Pit and fork → again. Follow the bridleway and single-track for 5km. Walk a short 30-metre section of private driveway before taking a ← onto the bridleway. **Howtown** is shortly followed by **Martindale** 1.25km later, with the impressive St Peter's Church on your right.

> In the case of **poor weather**, a low-level alternative for Stage 22 would be to head → towards Sandwick on a low-lying bridleway that will take you to Patterdale Valley without a high pass, instead of following the bridleway from Dale Head Farm out over Beda Fell.

St Peter's Church, Martindale

Stone leat

Route 1 – The Lakeland 200

22 ● Continue with the church on your right. Turn ← and descend through the hamlet and over a bridge. After 150 metres take a sharp ← onto a bridleway, signposted Winter Crag. Follow this for 1km keeping Howgrain Beck on your left until you rejoin the road. A farm at **Dale Head** is reached after another 2km. Beyond the farmyard, the path bears → towards the hill. Bedafell Knott is just visible above you to your right. The going here is unremitting hike-a-bike. After 1.5km the path tops out and briefly becomes rideable again. Boredale is below to your right. The wayfinding is tricky as a few paths intersect. Keep the hillock of Boredale Hause to your right and look for the car-wide track that will take you to the `A592`. This fast descent bottoms out into the valley floor to the left of the Goldrill Beck. A minor road takes you to a junction.

23 ◆ Turn ← into **Hartsop** and continue through the village onto a bridleway. Take the bridge over Hayswater Gill and follow the track up a steep hill until you have the stream on your left once more. Head ← over the footbridge and climb the slope until you reach **The Knott**, a rocky outcrop above you to the right.

24 ● The bridleway takes you behind the crag. Fork → and follow the Straits of Riggindale for 3.25km before taking a sharp ← at Thornthwaite Crag Beacon. Continue ↑ for 4.5km. Take a sharp ← over a river before turning → and continuing your descent south. Ignore the turnoff on your right to Limefitt Park and progress for 200 metres before taking a sharp ← onto Garburn Road (track).

25 ▲ Follow the track bearing → over the Garburn Pass until you drop into **Kentmere** village centre. With the church on your left, take a sharp →. At Kentmere Hall bear ←. Continue ↑ and climb out onto open fell before bearing →. At a fork, take the ← downhill until you cross Ullthwaite Bridge. Take the → and progress down the Kentmere Valley into **Staveley**.

2   41% off road

Route 2
Furness Forests

Start/finish	Oxenholme Lake District Railway Station
Total distance	103.3km (64 miles)
Off-road distance	44.4km
Percentage off-road	41%
Total ascent/descent	1890m
Grade	Moderate ●
Time	2–3 days
Terrain	Single-track 10%, track 31%, road 59%
Bike choice	Gravel/MTB

Introduction

The forests of High Furness offer the rider a tranquillity sometimes missing from the more popular destinations. The green lanes are secluded, the bridleways less trampled and the passes less demanding. This route explores the heart of Southern Lakeland via picturesque country lanes and ancient bridleways, and rewards you with one of longest and most stunning gravel descents in this guide.

Overview

The circuit begins and ends at Oxenholme, the Lake District Railway Station. After leaving the station take the back lanes towards Whitbarrow. Head down Winster Valley before climbing an ancient green lane over an exposed fell. A steep single-track descent through mature plantations finishes at Newby Bridge and shortly the route begins to wind along lanes and into High Furness. Grizedale Visitors Centre provides a welcome break before the route tackles a hard climb on single-track to High Parkamoor. From there the views on the descent to High Nibthwaite rival any in the Lakes. Now take the scenic route to Coniston along a series of bridleways and finally a lake-side cycle track. After Coniston head back

Coniston Water

over Monk Coniston Moor and back towards Grizedale Visitors Centre once more before taking a track through the forest to Satterthwaite. Next a steep climb arrives at plantation on single-track before the descent to Cunsey Beck and the road to the Windermere Ferry. Now on the eastern shore, take signs for Kendal before heading onto a series of green lanes that eventually lead back to Kendal and Oxenholme beyond.

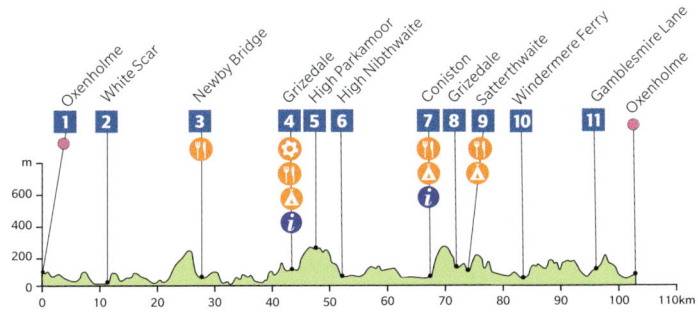

High Parkamoor green lane

Summary table

Waypoint	Section	Distance (km)	Ascent (m)	Descent (m)
1	Oxenholme – White Scar	12.2	100	180
2	White Scar – Newby Bridge	16.7	340	310
3	Newby Bridge – Grizedale	16.2	330	260
4	Grizedale – High Parkamoor	4.2	150	20
5	High Parkamoor – High Nibthwaite	3.5	0	180
6	High Nibthwaite – Coniston	14.1	130	150
7	Coniston – Grizedale	5.6	210	150
8	Grizedale – Satterthwaite	2.6	30	40
9	Satterthwaite – Windermere Ferry (west bank)	8.8	190	240
10	Windermere Ferry (east bank) – Gamblesmire Lane	12.4	270	210
11	Gamblesmire Lane – Oxenholme Station	7.0	140	150

Schedules

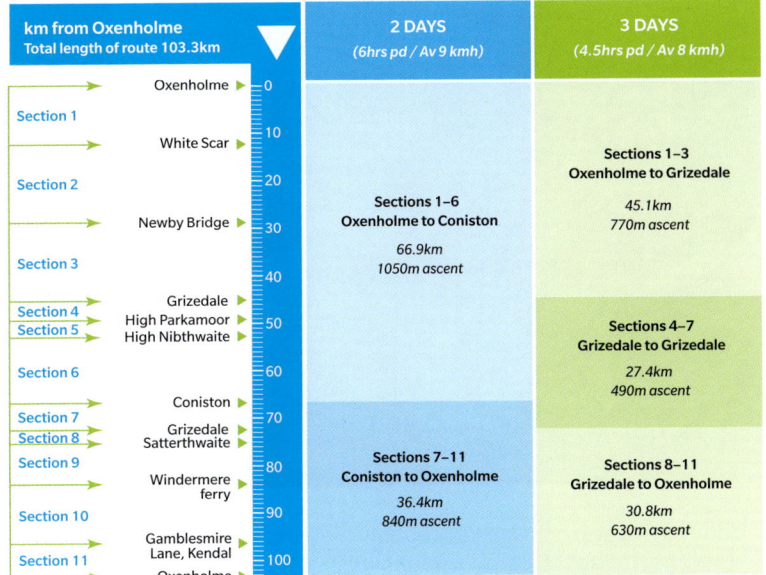

Surface	Grade	Description
paved	n/a	Quiet lanes on your way to the hills
mixed	▲	Mellow bridleways followed by steep single-track
paved	n/a	Country lanes all the way to the trail centre
unpaved	▲	Car-wide forestry road becomes steep single-track heading onto open fell
unpaved	▲	A stunning descent on a green lane with spectacular views
mixed	■	Quiet lanes are followed by off-road around an old reservoir before cycleways lead you into Coniston
unpaved	■	A bridleway through plantation with stunning views and a fast, easy descent
unpaved	■	A charming, undulating car-wide track through forest
unpaved	●	Tough single-track and hazardous bridleway takes you to the road and ferry beyond
mixed	■	Leave the main road behind and take country lanes to a bridleway. Occasionally tricky wayfinding
mixed	■	Take the old green lane over the hill and reconnect with minor roads before heading through Kendal into Oxenholme

Lakeland gravel

Alternative start/finish suggestions

If driving to the start of this route, you could park in Crosthwaite and join the route at Cowmire Hall 2km further south (Stage 2). On the return leg you would then fork → after Gilpin Mill (Stage 10). This would shorten the ride by approximately 30km. Alternatively, you could start in Windermere Train Station and follow the A592 to pick up the route at Newby Bridge, shortening the route by approximately 40km and making it possible to do the route in one long day.

Directions

1 Leave Oxenholme Lake District Station. Turn ← and follow the road round a corner and over a bridge before taking a sharp → onto Helmside Road. At the next junction turn → onto Burton Road. After 200 metres turn ← onto Oxenholme Lane and continue until **Natland**. Turn ←. After 400 metres, ignore a left signed Stanton and continue to **Sedgwick**. At Sedgwick bear → and progress under a railway bridge. Continue, then take a bridge on the right. Turn ← onto Force Ln. Take the path under the A591. Rejoin the road until it intersects with the busy A590. Cross the road. At the junction turn ← and continue uphill before descending through **Levens** passing right of the church. Opposite The Hare and Hounds pub, take a sharp → before turning ← over a bridge. Progress until the car showroom then take a →. Before

Route 2 – Furness Forests

reaching the A590 take the cycle path on the right. Continue over a bridge and rejoin a road. Turn → and head towards the hill of **White Scar**.

2 ▲ Take the first → towards Ravens Lodge. After entering the farmyard, follow the bridleway on the left until you rejoin a road. At the junction turn →. Maintain your direction past Witherslack Hall Equestrian Centre on your right. Progress through Pool Bank. At the next junction, fork ← signed for Bowland Bridge. After 200 metres pass the imposing Cowmire Hall on your left. A further 100 metres beyond this, take the ← and advance across the valley over Lobby Bridge. Ascend to Hodge Hill Hall and turn ← signed Lindale, Grange. Continue before taking the muddy Sow Lane on the right. Where two car-wide tracks intersect, cross and head through a gate. When you meet the road, turn ←. After 500 metres a gated road leads onto the fell. Take the first → and continue ↑. Bear → on a bridleway and head into Chapel House Plantation on single-track. First ascend and then descend through tall pines until you reach **Staveley-in-Cartmel**. Turn ← and then →, signed Ulverston/Newby Bridge, and head out of the village until you reach the A592. Turn ← and follow signs for Newby Bridge. Take the → over the bridge in **Newby Bridge**.

Watch out for branches on this challenging single-track

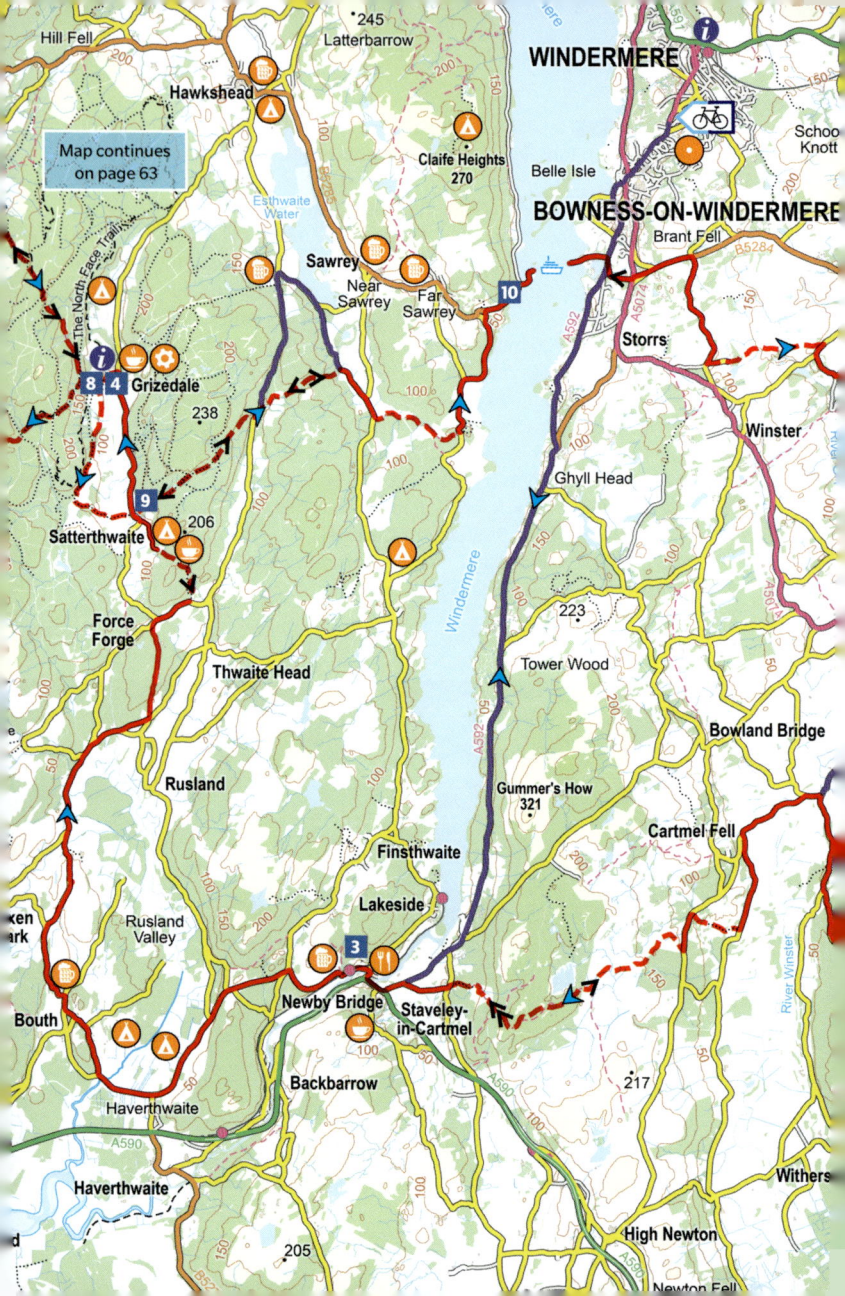

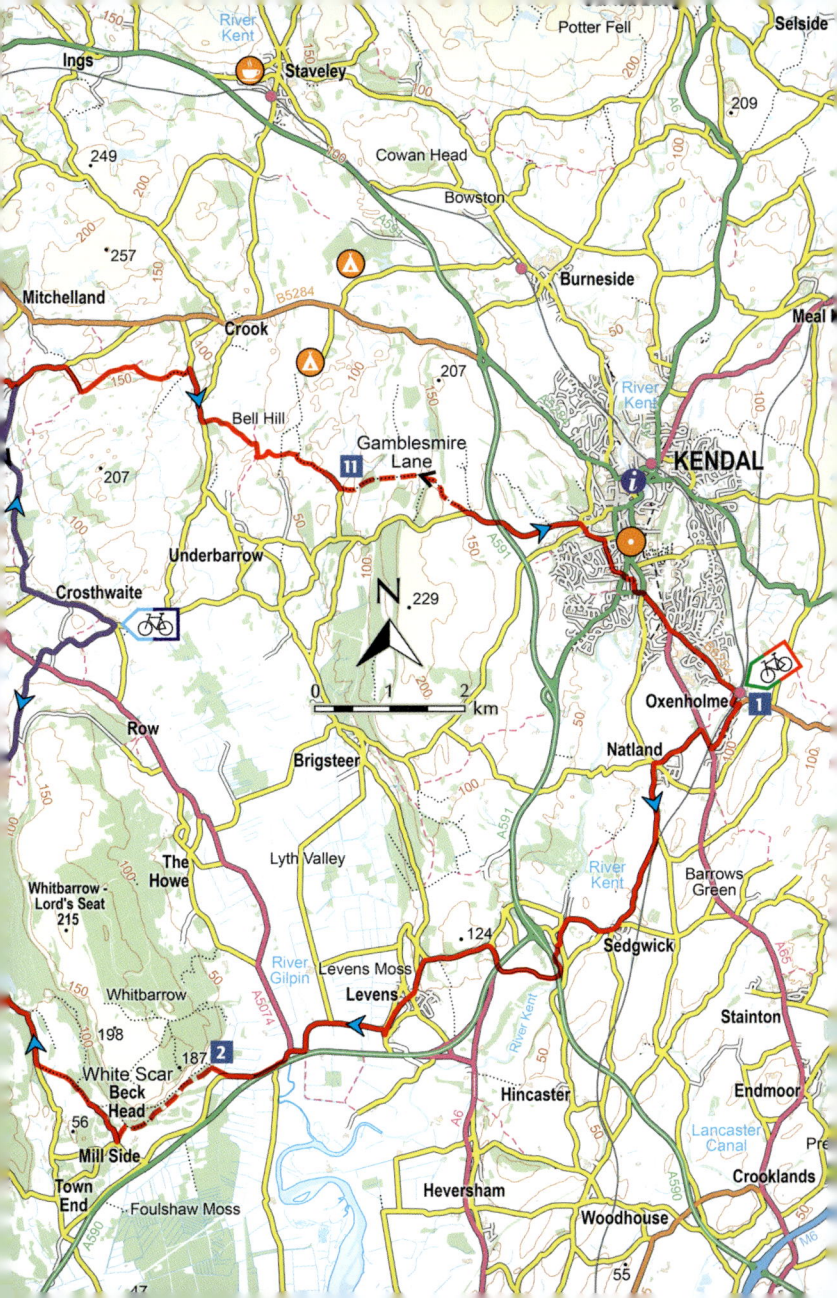

The Swan Hotel at Newby Bridge

3 Bear ← past the Swan Hotel, following signs for Haverthwaite. Progress over a railway bridge. At the staggered junction follow signs for Satterthwaite. Continue ↑. After Pool Bridge turn →, bypassing **Bouth** to the left, and climb north towards Burn Knott. Continue north bearing →. At Thwaite Moss take the cycleway to Force Mills. After the hamlet, take the bridleway on the left over Force Knott before descending into **Satterthwaite**. Follow the road up the valley to **Grizedale**.

> Grizedale is a mecca for mountain bikes and its visitor centre is reached twice on this route. It's a great place to get refreshments or visit a bike shop.

4 ▲ Keeping Grizedale Visitor Centre on your right, bear ← and descend to a bridge and through a gate before forking → and heading up the steep slopes into the forest. Numerous mountain bike trails criss-cross the forestry track. Your route is marked as a bridleway heading into the trees as a single-track. The narrow track intersects with forestry track and mountain bike trail as it slowly ascends into the open land south of the park, with a hill to your right. Near High Parkamoor the boggy bridleway meets a solid car track. Turn → here.

On route to Torver

5 ▲ The car-wide track descends slowly with stunning views to your right over the lake and towards the Old Man of Coniston beyond. The 3km-descent on a green lane to High Nibthwaite is one of the highlights in this guide.

6 ■ Turn ← on reaching the road. Continue for 1km before taking a →, signed Water Yeat/Torver. On reaching **Water Yeat** turn → and continue on the busy A5084 for 2km. Take the first ← over a small bridge. Continue for 1km before taking a bridleway on the right signed 'Torver, 2 miles'. Follow this along the right bank of the reservoir into Mill Bridge. Take the ← track before reaching the road. Continue on the bridleway until **Torver**. Before the junction take the bridleway on the right signed 'Coniston via lake shore'. The track takes you under a bridge and through a few gates then up onto a minor road before a descent to the lakeshore. Follow the cycle path until it meets the road into **Coniston**. Follow the cycle path through Coniston Park, passing Coniston Hall on your right. The path heads → and takes you to Lake Rd. Turn → and take the path that runs alongside the road before forking ← at the shore. Bear ← and follow the bridleway for 100 metres until it meets the B5285.

Route 2 – Furness Forests

7 ■ Turn → and continue around the northern shore of **Coniston Water**. Climb until you reach a junction. Turn → and continue for 300 metres. Take the bridleway on your left and ascend steeply as the path rises up into plantation, delivering stunning views back to Coniston. A long descent follows on single-track back towards Grizedale.

8 ■ Before reaching Grizedale take a bridleway on your right that runs along the slopes of the forest. After the climb, bear ← and descend into **Satterthwaite** once more.

> This route was ridden in early 2022, shortly after **two devastating storms** that affected most of the UK had torn through this area. The trees in the second half of Stage 9, after Slack Wood and into Devil's Gallop, had been badly damaged and made the bridleway impassable. We carried our bikes through the fallen trees. Hopefully by the time you read this the way will be open again. If you don't want to risk it, turn ← and head north on the road to Esthwaite Hall Bridge and then turn → where the road will shortly join back up to the route.

9 ● Join a steep bridleway heading north east out of the village through forest. The bridleway becomes single-track. Maintain your course when this intersects with forestry track. Climb and then descend until you finally meet the road. Turn ← and after 200 metres take a right. This is signed as a footpath but it's also a bridleway. Take the bridleway through the forest until you ascend to the road once more. Turn →. Continue for 1km. Take the bridleway on your left signed 'Low Cunsey 1 mile'. Follow this to Cunsey Bridge. Turn ← and progress until High Cunsey, bearing → and following the road parallel to the lake shore. Ascend and take the next →. Follow the signs for Windermere via ferry, and follow the road along the shore until you reach the ferry house on **Lake Windermere**. The ferry is usually cancelled in the event of bad weather, and the fare can only be paid by card.

10 ■ Cross to the marina and continue to the main road. Turn → at the T-junction with the A592 and then shortly turn ← and ascend on the B5284 signposted Kendal/Crook. After 1km turn → and descend to Lindeth Lane. After a further 1km take the green lane on your left for 1.5km. On meeting the road, turn → and then ← after 200 metres. Climb, then descend past Gilpin Mill and then after 300 metres turn ←. At the junction turn ← and climb up to Brow Head. Turn →. When the road runs out take the bridleway on your left and continue until you rejoin a road bearing ←. Ascend for 200 metres before taking a

Bikepacking in the Lake District

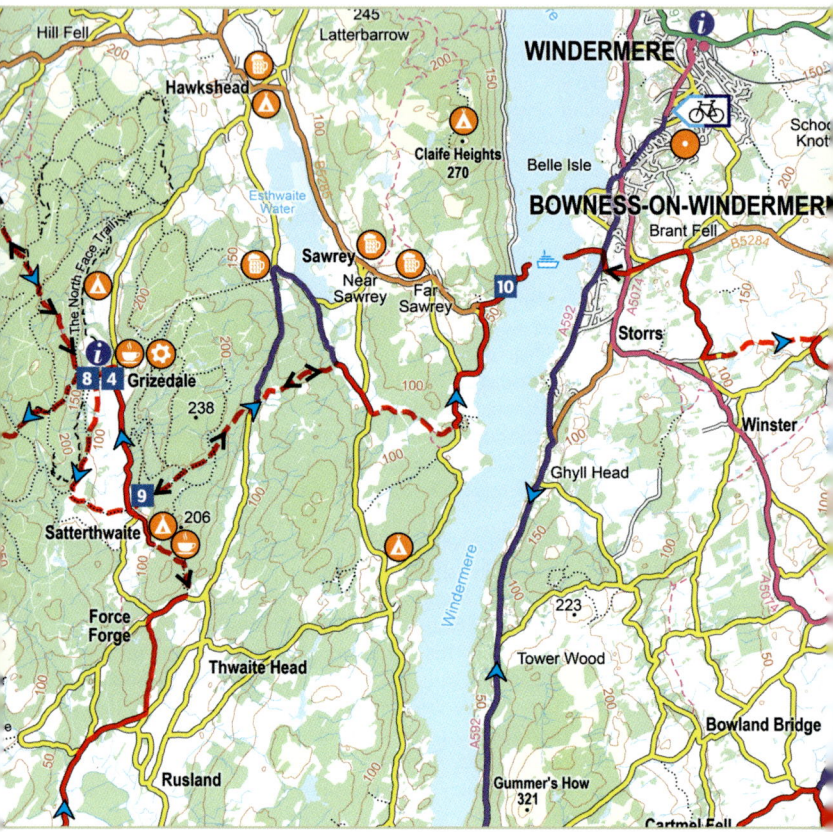

←, followed by a T-junction after 100 metres. Here turn → over Crag Hills. Continue and then take a green lane on the left to Beckside where the lane becomes a bridleway. After 400 metres the bridleway forks →. After a further 200 metres it forks ← before forking → and heading over fields. Ascend the track bearing →. Temporarily rejoin a road before reaching your goal of **Gamblesmire Lane**.

Route 2 – Furness Forests

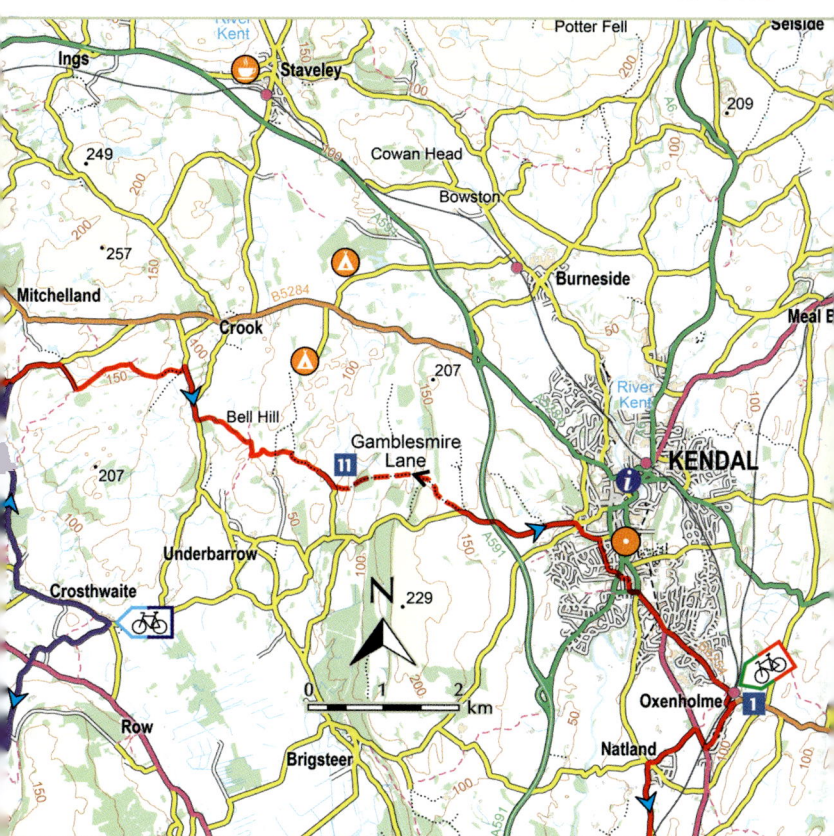

11 ■ Continue along the length of Gamblesmire Lane and enjoy the breathtaking views to your left back to the high fells in the north. Join Underbarrow Road and follow this over the bridge that spans the A591. Fork → as you head into **Kendal** before taking a further → through Kirkbarrow. At the main road turn → and then immediately ←. Head over Romney Bridge. Follow the A65 for a short distance before forking ← onto Oxenholme Road and heading up the hill to the station in **Oxenholme**.

3   40% off road

Route 3
The Old Man of Coniston and the Irish Sea

Start	Silecroft Railway Station
Finish	Foxfield Railway Station
Total distance	75.2km (46½ miles)
Off-road distance	31km
Percentage off-road	40%
Total ascent	2210m
Total descent	2210m
Grade	Hard ◆
Time	2–3 days
Terrain	Single-track 31%, track 9%, road 60%
Bike choice	Gravel/MTB

Introduction

An overwhelming sense of space greets you as your train slowly traverses the edge of Morecambe Bay from the county of Lancashire over the border to Cumbria. Your views are dominated by the Irish Sea to your left and the increasingly wild fells to your right. These windswept fells are reminiscent of the Pennines but they are a prelude to the main event: the Old Man of Coniston.

Overview

The bulk of the first day's hard work is done shortly after leaving Silecroft Station. Head straight up the nose of the famous Black Combe on a well-defined bridleway. From its summit, the views to the west out over the Irish Sea are matched by those to the east of the later challenge: the Old Man of Coniston. Follow a bridleway back to the road, then head up the western side of the massif before taking a rough bridleway to the remote and isolated Devoke Water. The descent that follows into

Morecambe Bay from the train

Dalegarth is magical. After the respite of picturesque Eskdale, climb round Harter Fell on good single-track before dropping down to a river crossing on stepping stones aided by a stout cable! The next prize, the Walna Scar Road, is deservedly famous and features in the Lakeland 200. From here drop into Torver on a steep bridleway. The final push goes along isolated fells and through plantation on quiet bridleways and exposed minor roads before arriving at Foxfield Station.

Bikepacking in the Lake District

Summary table

Waypoint	Section	Distance (km)	Ascent (m)	Descent (m)
1	Silecroft – Bootle	16.4	610	590
2	Bootle – Broad Oak	7.5	110	110
3	Broad Oak – Devoke Water	6.2	230	20
4	Devoke Water – Dalegarth Station	5.1	10	205
5	Dalegarth Station – Jubilee Bridge	4.1	80	15
6	Jubilee Bridge – Seathwaite Bridge	7.5	230	200
7	Seathwaite Bridge – Torver	8.1	450	500
8	Torver – Stephenson Ground	5.4	220	100
9	Stephenson Ground – Foxfield	14.9	270	470

Schedules

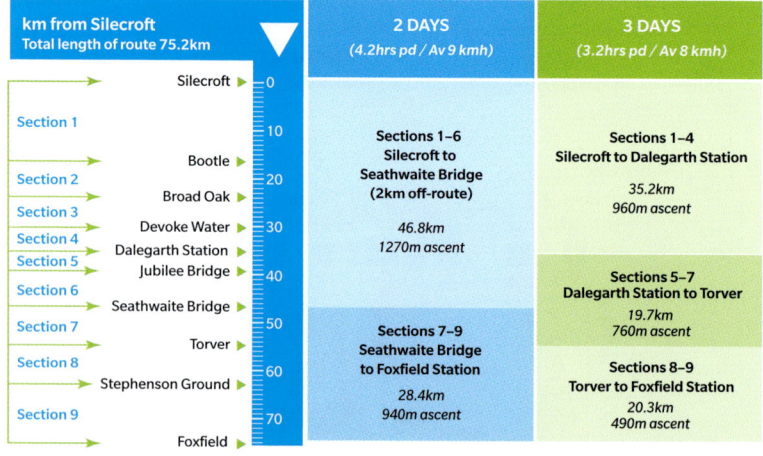

Route 3 – The Old Man of Coniston and the Irish Sea

Surface	Grade	Description
unpaved	●	Steep off-road climbing on well-defined path is rewarded by stunning views out to sea
paved	n/a	Quiet country roads link you to next off-road section
unpaved	▲	Rough bridleway leads to a remote and atmospheric lake
unpaved	■	Beautiful descent through wild landscape on good car-wide track
paved	n/a	Easy rolling along Eskdale Valley before the next challenge
unpaved	●	Hike-a-bike on well-defined single-track over Harter Fell to river crossing
unpaved	◆	Tough section over the shoulder of the Old Man of Coniston on car-wide track
mixed	■	Steep road climbing followed by easy forestry track
mixed	■	Exposed bridleway leads to gradual descent to train station

Alternative start/finish suggestions

This is the only route in the guide which starts and finishes at different locations. Both railway stations are on the same line and as the finish is closer to the main line, a return ticket to the start is still valid. You could consider starting the route at Dalegarth Railway Station having journeyed up Eskdale on the local train from Ravenglass. Alternatively, if arriving by car, parking in Broughton-in-Furness would offer a good starting location. This would give your legs a good warm-up before Black Combe but adds 7km to the start of the ride.

Directions

1 ● Leave the platform, turn ← over the level crossing and head north towards the hills. When you reach the A5093 turn ←. After 300 metres turn →, signed Barrow/Broughton. After 400 metres take a sharp ← and climb gradually towards a farm. When the road runs out take the bridleway which bears first ← then →. Now follow the steep but well-defined bridleway to the summit of **Black Combe**. With the steep scree slope on your → bear ← and follow the shoulder as it descends. Bear ← and follow the path to Whitbeck. Turn → and when you meet the road turn → onto the A595. Follow this to **Bootle**.

Route 3 – The Old Man of Coniston and the Irish Sea

2 Bear → and head through the town with the church on your right, signed Workington, Whitehaven, Gosforth. 300 metres beyond the church take a → over a stone bridge signed 'Corney 2, Unsuitable for HGVs'. Continue to **Corney**. Follow the road as it bears → and then ← before reaching a junction with an old red phone box. Turn → and climb to a junction then turn ←, signed Whitehaven, and continue to **Broad Oak**.

3 ▲ Continue through the hamlet of Broad Oak for a further 300 metres. On the right there is a wide concrete drive and three gates. Cross the cattle grid and take the ← fork, marked as a bridleway. Follow the bridleway through the farmyard and bear →. Climb gently before heading over a small bridge and bearing ← on a car-wide track flanked by stone walls. Continue and climb to a gate where the way forks, then take the →. Follow the often ill-defined bridleway as it leads you over **Birkby Fell** to **Devoke Water** then bears → around the lake.

4 ■ Close to the ancient boat house (built around 1772), the rough bridleway meets a good car-wide track. Follow this as it drops to the road. Opposite the track, follow the tarmac road signed Stanley Ghyll (road unfit for motors) as it descends into the valley. At the junction turn ←. After 20 metres the bridleway heads through the farmyard of High Ground, but the owners have requested

Devoke Water Boat House

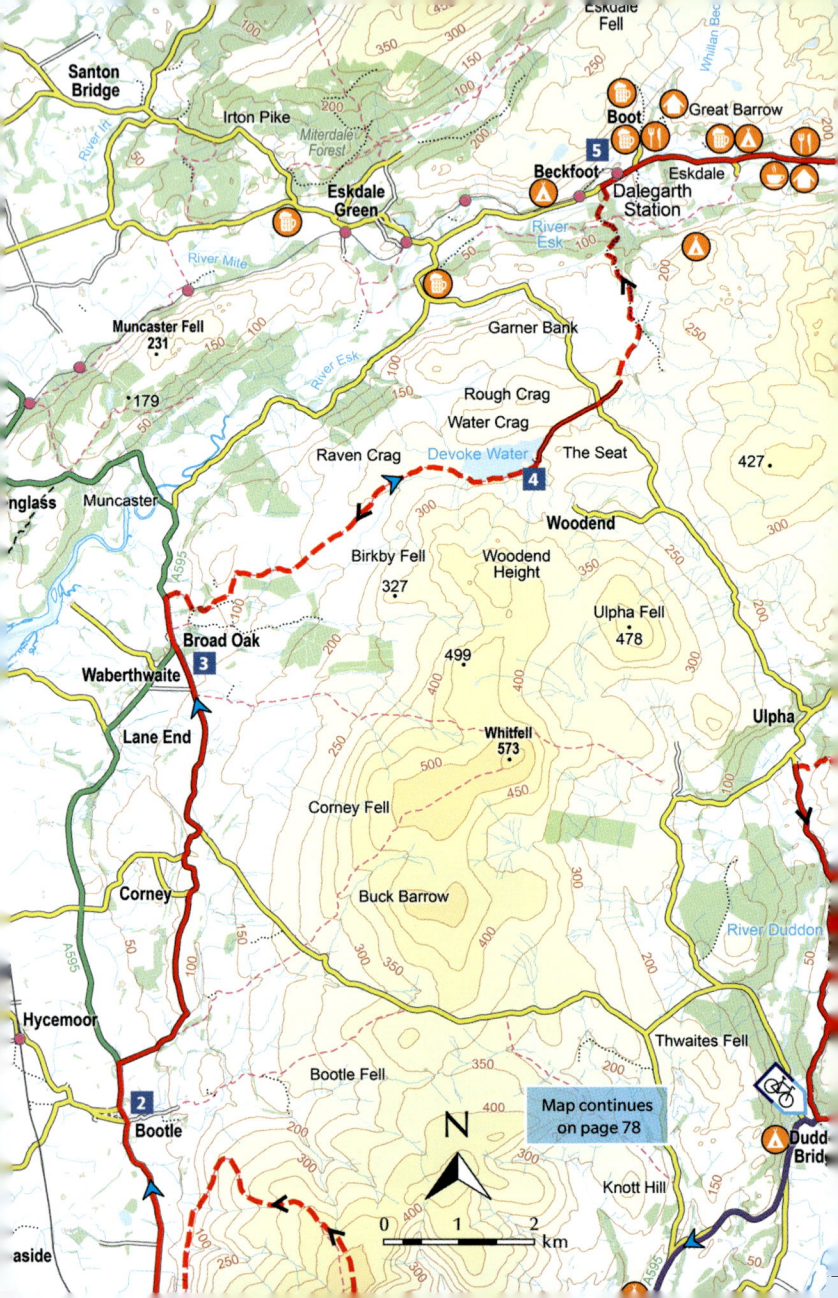

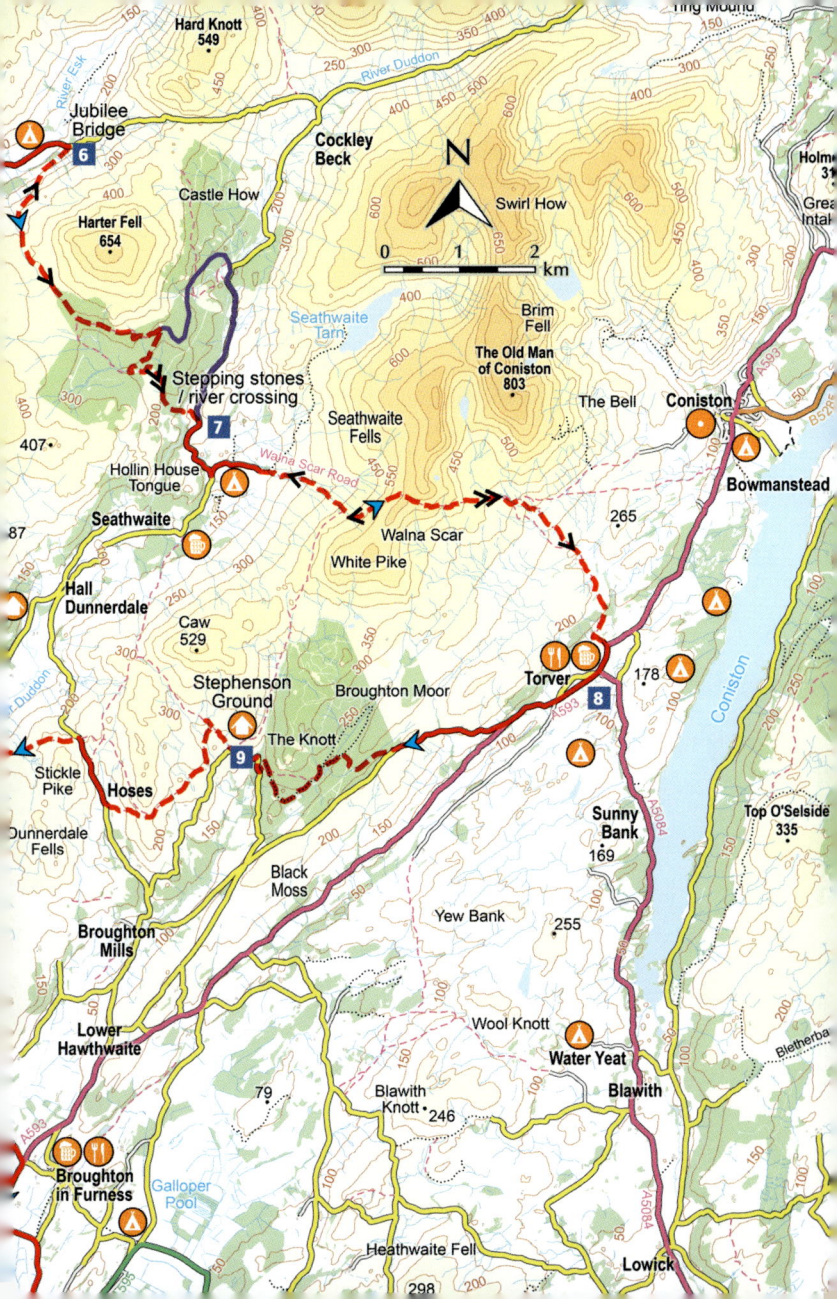

Bikepacking in the Lake District

people follow the path available around the farm. Descend on a car-wide track. At the junction fork ← and then climb past Low Ground Farm before continuing this stunning descent into Eskdale. The bridleway takes you past Dalegarth campsite before reaching the road. Turn right and continue to Dalegarth Station.

> **Eskdale** is home to three well-established campsites and the Eskdale YHA. Book ahead if you intend stopping here in the summer months.
>
> If you are looking to cut the tour short and need to head back towards the coast and the Northern Railway Line, then it's helpful to know the Dalegarth Railway Station is the final stop on the local Ravenglass Railway Line (bike spaces can be reserved on the website). It's also a great place to grab a snack before the challenging stages ahead. Alternatively, the Eskdale Trail is an off-road cycleway running for 8 miles parallel to the railway line to Ravenglass.

5 Continue east past **Dalegarth Station** along the valley to the foot of the infamous Hardknott Pass. Begin to climb through the woods. Immediately after you cross a cattle grid turn → onto a bridleway, signed 'Dunnerdale 3 miles', and cross the stone **Jubilee Bridge**.

Jubilee Bridge on route to Harter Fell

Route 3 – The Old Man of Coniston and the Irish Sea

An easy river crossing...when the river is low

> This next section ends with a **river crossing** on large stepping stones where you have to carry your bike. Outside of the summer months, you might want to avoid it and instead follow the forestry road to The Birks Outward Bound Centre and then on to the road. From there, turn right and continue until you rejoin the main route.

6 ● Good single-track takes you to the shoulder of **Harter Fell**. After a boggy stretch, enter the plantation. Ignore the fork to the right (Grassguards Gill is rough and boggy) and instead continue on forestry track for 200 metres before turning →. After 150 metres a sharp → takes you downhill. Bear ← then fork ← after wooden footbridge. Just before a ford (worth a look) a bridleway descends steeply into the forest. Unrideable at first, the wooded descent then opens up and delivers you to the river. Here you shoulder your bike and, holding a thick wire rope, cross on stepping stones. After reaching the far bank, haul your bike up the path and then ride to the road. Turn →.

7 ◆ After 1km of well-deserved road, climb to a junction and take the ← fork signposted 'Coniston Unfit for Cars'. The climb over the shoulder of the Old Man of Coniston is tough but spectacular. After 500 metres the road runs out. Now follow the **Walna Scar Road** as it climbs steeply. After heading through a gate by an old slate quarry bear ←. The climb gets steeper. Once you make the pass, the car-wide track descends into steep, rough single-track. After 500 metres of descent ignore the first bridleway on the right and head over Torver Bridge. Continue until a second bridleway on the right heads downhill to the left of the beck. Pass the discussed water-filled quarry on your right and after 100 metres turn → over a wooden footbridge. Turn ← and continue your

Bikepacking in the Lake District

Route 3 – The Old Man of Coniston and the Irish Sea

descent on a grassy car-wide track to the road and Scar Head. Follow the road as it bears ← before reaching a junction with the A593. Turn → and head into **Torver**. The Wilson's pub and the Torver Deli are good places to refuel.

8 ■ Continue on the A593 for 1km before turning → onto Old Rake and climbing steeply. Once over Hummer Bridge, continue for 400 metres before forking → onto a forestry track signposted Broughton Moor. Follow the forestry track and turn → then ← and ← again. Follow the track as it runs alongside the beck before bearing → and then forking →. At the next junction take a sharp ← and descend to the road. Turn → and continue over a picturesque stone bridge to stone buildings at **Stephenson Ground**.

> The impressive market town of **Broughton-in-Furness** is 1km off the route, but is well worth a visit if you are looking for a pub or tea shop to celebrate the ride's completion.

9 ■ Prior to Stephenson Ground farm and B&B, a gate on the right takes you onto the fell. After 150 metres the bridleway forks sharply ← downhill once more. Continue past Jackson Ground, along the edge of the fell, to Stainton Ground. Turn → when you reach the road and continue to ascend steeply past farm at **Hoses**. Opposite a small car park at the apex of the climb a vague track on your left takes you over the fell. Continue the descent for 1.5km on indistinct bridleway until you reach the road. Turn ← and begin a stunning descent that delivers you to **Duddon Bridge** after 5km. On meeting the A595 turn ← and follow this road for 3.5km to **Foxfield**.

4   23% off road

Route 4
Way Out in the Western Fells

Start/finish	Whitehaven Railway Station
Total distance	115.5km (72 miles)
Off-road distance	27km
Percentage off-road	23%
Total ascent/descent	2170m
Grade	Moderate ▲
Time	2–3 days
Terrain	Single-track 9%, track 14%, road 77%
Bike choice	Gravel/MTB

Introduction

The Western Fells are a special place. Far away from the hustle and bustle of Windermere or Ambleside, these steep, imposing hills frame two gems of Lakeland: Ennerdale and Buttermere. This route might put off the casual rider from outside the area – not because of the ride itself, technically one of the easier ones in this guide, but for its accessibility. Getting to the start requires a long journey on a branch line, either up from the south or down from Carlisle. But the rewards are worth it. Whitehaven has a lot of character and you really feel you are on the edge of the UK here.

Overview

From Whitehaven, the first few km rise up from the coast and soon the fells of Ennerdale and Loweswater are in sight. Pick up the NCN 71 and skirt along the far western edge of the national park. Continue on picturesque minor roads that hug the fell to Loweswater before following the NCN 71 along Lorton Valle to Low Lorton and the unmissable Wheatsheaf Inn. From there continue over the classic Whinlatter Pass and a fantastic single-track bridleway that intersects forestry tracks through pine plantation. Off-road NCN 71 follows, providing stunning

Rolling off the fell

views of Bassenthwaite Lake and mighty Skiddaw beyond. Next meet Wynthop, a high, secluded valley that feels like it's from a time out of mind, then return to Low Lorton and push south to Buttermere. The next off-road challenge goes along a wild bridleway between Gale Fell and Loweswater Fell. The descent that follows is one of the best in the guide. Continue along the western shore of Ennerdale through Ennerdale Bridge and over a classic road climb, Cold Fell, then it's a gentle warm-down through Egremont and St Bees before returning to the train station in Whitehaven.

Bikepacking in the Lake District

Summary table

Waypoint	Section	Distance (km)	Ascent (m)	Descent (m)
1	Whitehaven – Redbeck Road	8.5	160	90
2	Redbeck Road – Corpse Road	13.6	240	110
3	Corpse Road – Maggie's Bridge	4.2	30	110
4	Maggie's Bridge – Low Lorton	9.6	200	260
5	Low Lorton – Whinlatter Pass	5.3	260	20
6	Whinlatter Pass – Ladies Table	6.8	150	250
7	Ladies Table – Low Lorton	10.3	130	270
8	Low Lorton – Buttermere	11.3	160	120
9	Buttermere – Bowness Knott	11.0	350	330
10	Bowness Knott – Ennerdale Bridge	5.5	30	40
11	Ennerdale Bridge – Calder Abbey	10.4	200	220
12	Calder Abbey – Egremont	6.5	80	120
13	Egremont – St Bees	4.6	70	110
14	St Bees – Whitehaven	7.9	110	120

Crummock Water

Route 4 – Way Out in the Western Fells

Surface	Grade	Description
paved	n/a	A tough climb out of Whitehaven gifts you your first glimpse of the fells
paved	n/a	Take NCN 71 through quiet country lanes to the start of an ancient byway
unpaved	🟩	A magical off-road wooded descent
mixed	🟩	Traverse Fell Barrow on ancient green lanes
paved	n/a	A steady climb leads you to the trail centre
mixed	🔺	Breathtaking single-track descent is followed by a steady climb that takes you to a hidden valley
mixed	🟩	Descend along leafy lanes to Low Lorton
paved	n/a	Gentle cycling through a quintessential Lakeland valley
unpaved	🔺	A tough section over open fell rewards you with the best descent of the day
mixed	🟩	After a short road section head round the lake on a good track
paved	n/a	Climb out on a lonely fell with breathtaking views towards the coast
paved	n/a	A slow, gentle ascent to a market town
paved	n/a	Head towards the coast on minor roads
paved	n/a	The home straight into Whitehaven harbour

Schedules

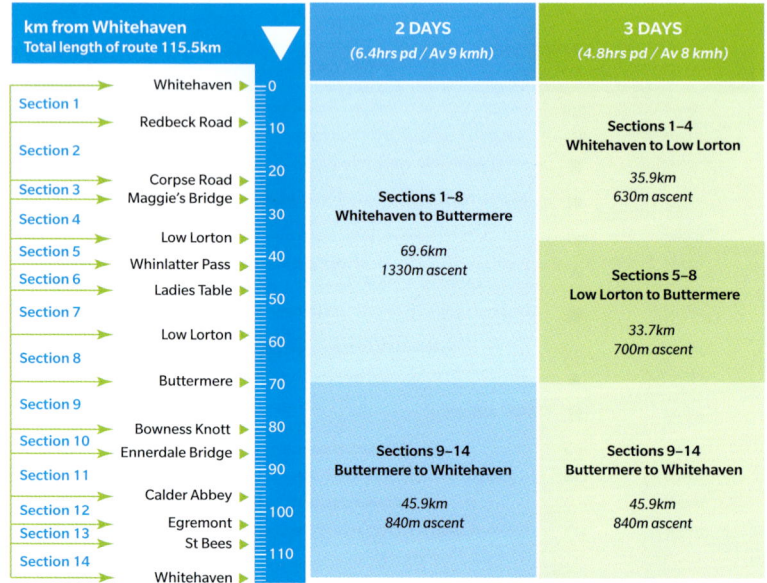

Alternative start/finish suggestions

Riders arriving by car could start in Keswick (joining close to Stage 6 at Thornthwaite, 5km west of Keswick) and begin to turn back at Ennerdale Bridge (Stage 10). This removes close to 25km from the route.

Directions

1 Leave Whitehaven Railway Station and continue past the petrol station on the left and turn ➔. Take the next ⬅ and, after 100 metres, turn ⬅ onto Wellington Row. Ascend steeply and bear ➔ under a bridge and onto Harras Road. Continue to a roundabout. Take the second exit signed Cleator Moor/Hensingham. Continue to a junction with a fire station on the right and turn ⬅, signed Cleator Moor 2½. Follow this road through the town to the A5086, signed Frizington Rd and adjacent to the church. Turn ⬅ here. After 200 metres turn ➔ onto **Redbeck Road** (unsuitable for HGVs).

Route 4 – Way Out in the Western Fells

2 You are now heading towards the fells. Continue on Redbeck Road until a crossroads. With Kirkland CE Academy on your right, turn →. Progress through the village of **Kirkland** and over the junction, taking signs for Croasdale. Follow the road until a T-junction. Keltonfell is ahead of you. Turn ← and join the **NCN 71**. Continue through Felldyke and bear ← past Inglenook Caravan Park. Climb slowly to **Lamplugh**. St Michael's Church in Lamplugh and the stone entrance arch to Lamplugh Hall are worth a short stop. The mediaeval gargoyles on the spire are quite elaborate. Bear ← before turning →, signed Loweswater 2½. Continue as the road bears → uphill before views of the fell open up to your right. Look for the bridleway on the right leading to **Old Corpse Road**.

Old Corpse Road towards Loweswater

3 ■ The bridleway is gained through a gate on the right. Follow the stony car-wide track towards the fell. After 200 metres head through a gate on the left signed Watergate Farm. Follow this bridleway, bearing → past Iredale Place, as it drops down through the fields. Cross the farmyard at Hudson Place and head through a gate marked 'Footpath'. Continue on the bridleway through the woods, fording small streams with Loweswater on your left. At Watergate Farm follow the bridleway onto open land and on to **Maggie's Bridge** and the junction with Fangs Brow Road beyond.

4 ■ Turn ←. Follow the road for 600 metres until a green lane on your right leads you around the shoulder of **Darling Fell**. Climb on this car-wide track before descending once more and meeting with the road. Continue through a farmyard to a junction. Take signs for Cockermouth then head into **Mosser**. Ignore two left turns before forking ←, signed Cockermouth, in the centre of the hamlet. After 300 metres turn → over a stone bridge onto a second green lane. Continue on this until it meets back up with the road and drops you into **Low Lorton**. The Wheatsheaf pub at Low Lorton is one of the few in the area and it's a gem. Friendly staff, nice beer garden and excellent fare.

Route 4 – Way Out in the Western Fells

5 With the imposing walls of Lorton Hall on your left turn → and then shortly fork ← signed Keswick 8½ . Continue ↑ to High Lorton. Fork →, signed Boonbeck/Scales, and cross a small bridge and began the climb to **Whinlatter Pass**. After 2km of climbing, join the B5292 and shortly afterwards head over the pass itself.

6 ▲ Shortly after the pass take a ← signed Whinlatter Forest Park. Continue ↑ bearing → and leave the car park at the rear of the complex. Take the bridleway which drops into the forest. The descent is challenging in part as it drops on rocky single-track through the conifers and over wooden bridges. Cross the car-wide track and drop sharply with the beck on your right until you meet tarmac once more. Continue and bear ←, skirting **Thornthwaite** before rejoining the NCR71. Continue north until you get close to the A66. Prior to this busy road, take the auxiliary road on your left signed NCR71. Follow this as it forks ← again onto a bridleway. Climb through tall conifers to the brow of the hill below **Ladies Table**. Wythop is a special place, remote, elevated and very beautiful.

Climb onto Ladies Table (with Skiddaw in the background)

Bikepacking in the Lake District

7 ■ The bridleway continues through the field. Take the ← fork which reaches a minor road after 600 metres. Continue ↑ bearing ← and hugging the shoulder of Ling Fell. Take the Green Lonning bridleway on the left and bear ← out of Highside Farm onto a minor road and over a stone bridge. Descend to a junction, turn ← and continue on to a second junction where the minor road meets the B5292. Turn ←. After 500 metres take the → fork signposted Low Lorton, Loweswater, Buttermere.

8 On reaching **Low Lorton** turn → at the green, signposted Low Lorton, Loweswater, Buttermere. After 200 metres turn ← and then immediately ← signposted Thackwaite, Rogerscale. Continue with a high stone wall on your right. Cross the bridge and then take the ← signed Thackwaite. Now you are on the NCN 71. Continue south through Thackwaite for 4km. As the road ascends, take the ← fork and continue to the crossroads signposted Loweswater. Here turn ← and descend briefly before crossing a bridge. Head through the car park on the right and onto a bridleway. Continue on this for 1km before turning → onto the B5289. Continue with Crummock Water on your right until you reach **Buttermere**.

> The second half of Stage 9 is **the toughest and highest part of the route**. You follow a bridleway that snakes up a small valley and over two passes. This will take two hours. It's hike-a-bike and occasionally marshy.

9 ▲ After passing The Bridge Hotel turn → and head through the carpark. On the left side of the carpark, beyond Buttermere Court Hotel, head through a gate signed Scale Bridge. When the track forks, a gate on the right gives access to a

Some hard work to do after Buttermere

path running along the side of a field. Continue and head over Scale Bridge. Turn → onto a rough bridleway. The track fords a few streams and meanders as it bears ←. The first pass delivers you to a wild fell. Here, bear ← and drop down and head over a stream. Your object is in sight: a pass between Gale Fell and Whiteoak Moss. The bridleway is sometimes ill-defined and there are also footpaths crossing it. Head through a gate and haul yourself up a steep path running to the right of a wall. Top out at Floutern Cop. The single-track that follows is great fun and the views are outstanding. At the first fork bear → and at the second take a sharp ← onto a narrow path between a wall and a hedge. When you reach the road turn ← and continue up towards Ennerdale beneath **Bowness Knott** until you reach a car park.

10 ■ Here take the → fork onto the bridleway that takes you to the lake. On reaching the lake, stop for a swim or alternatively turn → and follow the gravel track that borders the lake until you reach a weir. Turn → and follow the bridleway to a minor road. At the junction fork ← and continue into **Ennerdale Bridge**. Consider stopping at the Gather Tea Rooms in the village of Ennerdale Bridge; this is a great pit stop before the climb up to Cold Fell.

11 Shortly after Ennerdale turn ← and begin the climb to Cold Fell. Follow the exposed minor road as it climbs steeply at first before levelling off. Continue over high exposed fell on paved road and pass **Cold Fell** before descending steeply.

Route 4 – Way Out in the Western Fells

12 The road bears L but you need to take a → signed Haile 1½ . At the T-junction turn → and continue to **Haile** then take a ← signed Egremont 2½. Bear ← and continue to the town. At the roundabout take the second exit signed Egremont/Nethertown.

13 Head over the bridge and into **Egremont**. In the town centre turn ←, signed St Bees/Nethertown. Head out of the town on Grove Rd towards St Bees.

14 Coming into **St Bees** on Outrigg Place, turn → at the junction and continue your descent into the town. As the road levels out head over a railway crossing before climbing uphill on the B5345. Take the ← fork onto Byerstread Rd and continue to a junction. Turn ← following the NCN 72. Continue into the outskirts of **Whitehaven**. Turn → when High Road meets Harbour View Rd and turn ← onto Wellington Lodge. Descend on the cycleway past The Wellington Inn car park. When you meet West Strand, turn → before taking a ← onto the Old Quay. Wheel your bike over the Whitehaven Sea Lock and onto the marina. Continue to your → and then take a ← with Tesco visible in front of you. Turn → and then ← and head across Tesco car park before turning ← towards Whitehaven Station.

Stunning descent from Floutern Cop

5 50% off road

Route 5
Helvellyn and Back

Start/finish	Windermere Railway Station
Total distance	95.9km (59½ miles)
Off-road distance	48km
Percentage off-road	50%
Total ascent/descent	2440m
Grade	Hard ◆
Time	2–3 days
Terrain	single-track 14%, track 36%, road 50%
Bike choice	MTB

Introduction

This route boasts the greatest number of superlatives of any in this guide. The route includes the highest navigable MTB route in England, the greatest distance-to-ascent ratio of the routes, the third highest pub in England and the third hardest road climb in the guide. It also includes arguably the most dramatic landscape, the best Lakeland views and the most thrilling single-track descent. There are great camping spots and fantastic places to eat, and it has easy access by train. The route takes you from the heart of Lakeland, Windermere, to the summit of the third highest mountain in England before returning via the Cumbria Way through Langdale and making use of the ferry.

Overview

Leave Windermere Railway Station and quickly join ancient bridleways to Ambleside. Struggle up The Struggle road climb to Kirkstone Pass before a 10km descent into Patterdale. Enjoy the ascent into Grisedale and then hike-a-bike to the tarn. A brutal hike-a-bike finishes at Dollywagon Pike and then it's easy going to the main peak: Helvellyn. Descend via Sticks Pass to Legburthwaite and then take the A591 5km towards Keswick. Turn south and hug the shore of Derwent

Route 5 – Helvellyn and Back

Water to Rosthwaite before leaving the road for the Cumbria Way. Rocky going is rewarded with an easy climb to Stake Pass. The descent that follows down Black Crags is one of the best in the Lakes. The final warm-down section follows hardpack tracks and the off-road NCN 6 route to the Windermere Ferry and finally to the station on the eastern shore.

Alternative start/finish suggestions

If arriving by car you could start and finish the route in Ambleside: start the route at Stage 2 and end at Stage 12, heading directly to Ambleside from Skelwith Bridge. This would take 20km off the length of the ride. I would not suggest reversing the route.

Getting the coffee on

Schedules

km from Windermere Total length of route 95.9km		2 DAYS (6hrs pd / Av 9 kmh)	3 DAYS (4.5hrs pd / Av 8 kmh)
Section 1	Windermere Railway Station — 0		Sections 1–3 Windermere Railway Station to Patterdale 24.2km 1020m ascent
Section 2	Ambleside — 10	Sections 1–8 Windermere Railway Station to Legburthwaite 41.6km 1540m ascent	
Section 3	Kirkstone Pass — 20		
Section 4	Patterdale		
Section 5 Section 6 Section 7	Grisedale Tarn — 30 Dollywagon Pike Helvellyn		Sections 4–10 Patterdale to Rosthwaite 34.9km 1090m ascent
Section 8	Sticks Pass Legburthwaite — 40		
Section 9			
Section 10	Keswick — 50	Sections 9–14 Legburthwaite to Windermere Railway Station 54.3km 900m ascent	
Section 11	Rosthwaite — 60		Sections 11–14 Rosthwaite to Windermere Railway Station 36.8km 690m ascent
Section 12	Stake Pass — 70		
Section 13	Skelwith Bridge — 80		
Section 14	Windermere Ferry — 90 Windermere Railway Station		

Bikepacking in the Lake District

Summary table

Waypoint	Section	Distance (km)	Ascent (m)	Descent (m)
1	Windermere Railway Station – Ambleside	10.4	220	280
2	Ambleside – Kirkstone Pass	4.8	390	0
3	Kirkstone Pass – Patterdale	9.0	10	315
4	Patterdale – Grisedale Tarn	6.7	400	25
5	Grisedale Tarn – Dollywagon Pike	1.4	270	0
6	Dollywagon Pike – Helvellyn	2.5	160	20
7	Helvellyn – Sticks Pass	3.9	90	290
8	Sticks Pass – Legburthwaite	2.9	0	570
9	Legburthwaite – Keswick	7.7	70	150
10	Keswick – Rosthwaite	9.8	140	130
11	Rosthwaite – Stake Pass	7.8	390	10
12	Stake Pass – Skelwith Bridge	14.3	90	510
13	Skelwith Bridge – Windermere Ferry (west bank)	11.2	130	140
14	Windermere Ferry (east bank) – Windermere Station	3.5	80	0

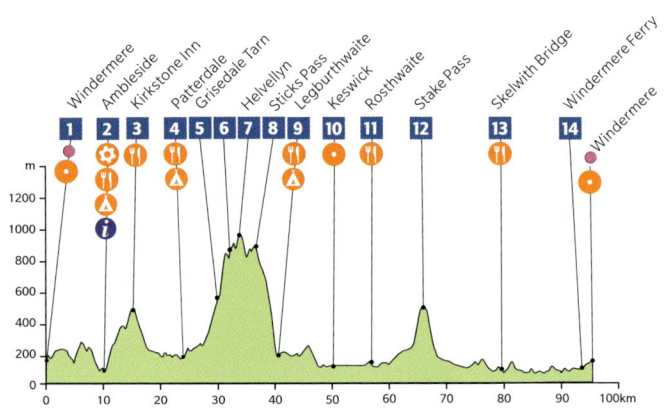

Route 5 – Helvellyn and Back

Surface	Grade	Description
Mixed	●	Ancient bridleways afford stunning views of Lake Windermere and a challenging single-track descent
paved	n/a	The Struggle lives up to its name
paved	n/a	Welcome descent to the foot of the climb
mixed	●	A stunning valley ride gives way to hike-a-bike to the tarn
unpaved	◆	Brutal gradients before topping out brings relief
unpaved	▲	Easy off-road over wide ridge
unpaved	●	Tricky at first then easy to the pass
unpaved	▲	Straightforward descent leads to hike-a-bike on final section
paved	n/a	A road with good hard shoulder
paved	n/a	Flank Derwent Water to the village
unpaved	▲	Follow the Cumbria Way on rough ground along the valley floor before straightforward climb to the pass
mixed	●	An amazing descent is followed by a relaxing warm-down along valley floor
unpaved	■	Easy rolling on off-road NCN route 6 to the ferry terminal
paved	n/a	Climb through the town to the train

Directions

1 ● Leave the station precinct and turn → onto the A591. Continue for 800 metres before taking a ← signed 'Unsuitable for HGVs and Coaches'. Continue on this shallow climb over the first junction until you reach Moorhowe Road. Turn ← and follow Fusethwaite Ln until it reaches the A592 then turn →. Descend for 100 metres before heading through a gate on the left and down a steep gravel descent and over a large wooden footbridge. Climb the green lane to the road. Head directly through the adjacent gateway into what looks like a private drive. This steep bridleway meets a road. Turn ← and then almost immediately → onto another bridleway. Now climb past a stone barn on your right and on to Robin Lane. Stunning views towards Lake Windermere to the left are to be had as you follow an undulating car-wide track. The track then heads through woodland and delivers a technical descent before meeting

Looking back on The Struggle

asphalt once more. Prior to meeting the A591 and the one-way system, take a sharp → onto a road running parallel to the main street.

2 In **Ambleside** town centre take the →, North Road, prior to the war memorial. Follow this cut-through before turning → into Kirkstone Road. Climb on this before taking the ← fork onto The Struggle. Follow this steep category 2 hill climb for 4.5km until you arrive at Kirkstone Pass and the A592.

3 On reaching the busy A592 turn ← and head past the third highest pub in England, **The Kirkstone Inn**, before descending for 5km and continuing to **Patterdale**.

> The main object of this route is the mountain **Helvellyn**, the third highest peak in England and the highest location you can legitimately take a mountain bike in England. There are two access points to choose from on the Ullswater side. This route favours the Grisedale ascent because it takes you via Grisedale Tarn and Dollywagon Pike and you then continue north. However, this is not the easiest route up. An alternative, the Keppel Cove ascent, is shorter and keeps the rider on a rideable track for

Bikepacking in the Lake District

> longer before the inevitable hike-a-bike – but if this second access point is used, a further short and brutal hike-a-bike south stands between the rider and the peak. You also miss out on the stunning Grisedale Valley and the dramatic tarn.

4 ● Continue through Patterdale before taking a ← signed 'Lane to Grisedale, no public parking'. Follow this narrow road as it runs parallel to the beck for 2km. When the road runs out, follow the track. When this runs out, continue on the path. It's hike-a-bike to Ruthwaite Lodge (climbing hut). The path deteriorates further as you climb to the tarn.

5 ◆ From the shore of the tarn you can see what lies between you and the summit: 200 metres of almost vertical ascent over 1km. The path is a solid construction of large stone steps, so it doesn't feel precarious. It is, however, very steep.

Heading up Grisedale

Route 5 – Helvellyn and Back

Topping out on Dollywagon will put a smile on your face

6 ▲ The relief as you start to top out on **Dollywagon Pike** is palpable. Follow the obvious track on the broad ridge north to **Nethermost Pike**. From there descend before climbing again to **Helvellyn** itself at 950m.

7 ● After catching your breath and (hopefully) enjoying the view from the summit, pick your way slowly down **Lower Man** and climb on the open ridge to White Side. Bear → and head over Raise. You can see the junction of Sticks Pass below you; enjoy the descent.

8 ▲ At **Sticks Pass** turn ←. Follow the track off the mountain to **Legburthwaite** and the A591.

> The area around **Thirlmere** has a few welcome opportunities for the rider. There's a great camping barn here, Fisher Gill Barn, and also The Kings Head Inn and a campsite at Thirlspot. All are recommended.

9 Follow the A591 north towards Keswick for 5km. There are no quieter alternatives without heading over the fell. Outside **Keswick** take a ← onto Manor Brow, signed Castlerigg Manor.

Bikepacking in the Lake District

10 Manor Brow becomes Ambleside Road. Turn ← at Church Lane and take the cycle path. Turn ← onto Borrowdale Road. This becomes the B5289 and you continue on this uninterrupted for 8km to **Rosthwaite**.

> **Rosthwaite** is a small, picturesque village that acts as the gateway to Borrowdale. There is a tea room called The Flock-in (cash only), a hotel, and a YHA. This is your last chance for refreshments before reaching Great Langdale, 13km and 400m of climbing later.
>
> The next section follows **the Cumbria Way** on a bridlepath. There is a better, less lumpy, track on the other side of Langstrath Beck. After 2km this becomes a footpath so cannot be ridden, but there's nothing to prevent you from pushing your bike along here. Before the beck forks, there is a footbridge to deliver you back to the east bank before the Stake Pass ascent. This pass is a joy after the previous day's efforts and the descent is exceptional.

11 ▲ Just prior to the village take a ←, then cross a bridge and take a track on the right signposted Cumbria Way. Ignore the first right towards Stonethwaite. After a further 1km take a → over a footbridge. Continue on this occasionally

Into Langstrath Valley on route to Stake Pass

The source of Stake Gill

boulder-strewn path for 3km. When the valley forks, bear ←. Cross a wooden bridge and then begin to climb on a good, even, path as it zig-zags uphill. The views back along Langstrath are breathtaking.

12 ● After making the pass, follow the path for 100 metres over Langdale Combe before taking a → fork and beginning your descent. Follow the technical single-track that zig-zags down Black Crags until you reach the wooden bridge that spans the beck on the valley floor. Now continue down the sublime Mickleden valley until you reach the **Old Dungeon Ghyll Hotel** car park beyond Middle Fell Farm. Follow the road over a stone bridge. Turn ← and continue for 1km. Head through a car park on the right and take the hardpack car-wide track. At the gate turn →, then → again. Cross the bridge, fork → and follow the bridleway into Hag Wood on NCN 37. Head into **Elterwater**. After the stone bridge take a → signed Cumbria Way. Follow this before turning → onto the B5343. Continue to **Skelwith Bridge**.

> It's worth **checking your timings** at this stage. Check the ferry times and also those of the train you are heading for to make sure you have time to make your connection if you catch the ferry. If time is tight, take the less pleasant A593/A591 route to Windermere via Ambleside.

13 ■ Turn → over the bridge. Follow the road and climb steeply to Skelwith Fold, then continue to climb bearing →, signed Hawkshead. After 200 metres take an unsigned ← on a car-wide asphalt drive to Holmeshead Farm. Continue beyond the farm downhill to the road. Turn ← then at the junction turn →. After 300 metres the road bears right but you need to take a ← onto an off-road NCN route 6 that delivers you to the shore of **Windermere**. Follow this for 6km until you reach the **ferry terminal** (card only at the time of writing).

14 On the east bank of the lake follow the auxiliary road until you meet the A592. Windermere Railway Station is not well signed. Turn ← and follow this for 1km before turning ← and then taking the → fork for 1.5km up the hill and through the centre of the town on the A5074. Turn → and continue to the station precinct in **Windermere**.

6 40% off road

Route 6
Dalston/Skiddaw Mega Pretzel

Start/finish	Dalston (Cumbria) Railway Station
Alternative start/finish	Millhouse
Alternative finish	Penrith Railway Station
Total distance	123.5km (76½ miles)
Off-road distance	51km
Percentage off-road	40%
Total ascent/descent	2040m
Grade	Hard ●
Time	2–3 days
Terrain	Single-track 14%, track 26%, road 60%
Bike choice	Gravel/MTB

Introduction

The Skiddaw Massif has a unique character that sets it apart from its more southerly neighbours. Although impressive from any angle, its awe-inspiring bulk is perhaps best appreciated from the western shores of Bassenthwaite Lake. More than anywhere else in the Lake District, this feels like the remotest parts of the Scottish Highlands. At 931m, Skiddaw is the fourth highest peak in the Lakes. This route takes advantage of the three cyclable routes onto the massif. Each has a distinct flavour and each affords the rider breathtaking views.

The track to Skiddaw House

Overview

Begin from the branch line station of Dalston, the first stop on the Northern Train Line if heading south from Carlisle. Follow the NCN 7 south along the Caldew Valley through pretty villages until picking up the Cumbria Way and then continuing on the NCN 10 (aka the Reivers Off-road Route). Hug the western flank of the Skiddaw Massif, keeping Bassenthwaite Lake on the R, before climbing on minor roads to a car park. Here, meet the Cumbria Way (CW) and follow it to Skiddaw House YHA. The route then continues east on the Cumbria Way to Mosedale before forking north east and hugging the shoulders of Caldbeck and Uldale fells on mixed NCN to Peter House Farm. The second ascent of the mountain begins from its north-west flank. Join up with the Cumbria Way once more and pass the YHA again, this time arriving from the north. Drop down to Threlkeld and pick up the NCN 71, going north around the south-eastern shoulder before returning on exposed minor roads to the NCN 10 and 7 and the final lanes before Dalston.

Bikepacking in the Lake District

Summary table

Waypoint	Section	Distance (km)	Ascent (m)	Descent (m)
1	Dalston – Raughton Head	6.0	70	10
2	Raughton Head – Caldbeck	11.0	150	90
3	Caldbeck – Bassenthwaite	14.5	290	355
4	Bassenthwaite – Gale Road car park	11.4	280	90
5	Gale Road car park – Skiddaw House	5.6	180	15
6	Skiddaw House – Mosedale	8.8	0	240
7	Mosedale – Calebreck	4.0	90	10
8	Calebreck – Fell Side	5.3	160	170
9	Fell Side – Longlands	4.5	80	150
10	Longlands – Peter House Farm	4.4	80	90
11	Peter House Farm – Skiddaw House	5.6	290	40
12	Skiddaw House – Threlkeld	6.7	30	340
13	Threlkeld – Mungrisdale	7.9	140	60
14	Mungrisdale – Hesket Newmarket	11.4	100	160
15	Hesket Newmarket – Dalston	16.4	100	220

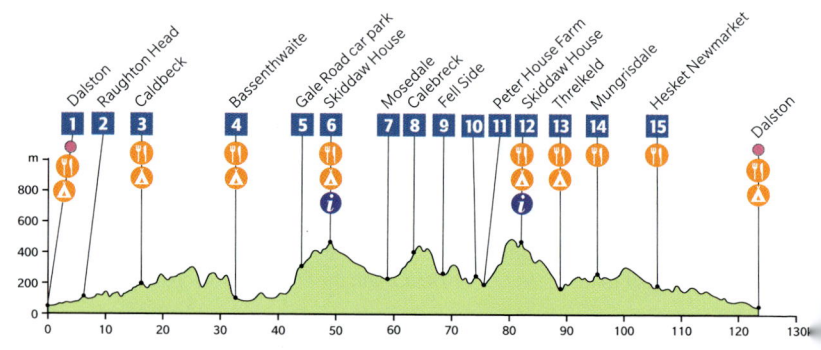

Route 6 – Dalston/Skiddaw Mega Pretzel

Surface	Grade	Description
paved	n/a	A gentle start on NCN 10, the Reivers Off-road Route, and the Cumbria Way
mixed	n/a	Off-road on good car-wide track to rejoin a wooded section of the Cumbria Way
mixed	■ (green)	With Skiddaw in view, skirt west on a lonely road over the open fell before the Reivers Off-road Route takes you to Bassenthwaite
paved	n/a	A spur of the NCN 10 is followed by 2km of fast road before you fork ← and begin your climb
unpaved	● (red)	Off-road on breathtaking single-track to the highest hostel in England
mixed	▲ (blue)	Descend the Caldew Valley on great single-track to the hamlet of Mosedale
paved	n/a	Skirt east of the massif on quiet lanes
unpaved	■ (green)	Head over open fell on rough car-wide track with stunning views
mixed	■ (green)	NCN 10 becomes the Reivers Off-road Route and delivers you to Longlands
paved	n/a	The route follows the Cumbria Way and then the NCN 10 through quiet hamlets
unpaved	▲ (blue)	A gentle climb gives way to a more challenging ascent past the Dash Falls
unpaved	▲ (blue)	Perfect fast single-track descent skirting Blease Fell
mixed	■ (green)	Easy cycle paths followed by lanes to the east of the massif
paved	n/a	Quiet roads to a picturesque village
paved	n/a	NCN 10 and 7 back to Dalston

Alternative start/finish suggestions

The standard start/finish location is Dalston Railway Station. However, if you are journeying to the start by car, Millhouse – 3km east of Hesket Newmarket – is a good location to start from. There is a campsite close by where you could camp the night before setting out and then leave your car. This option shortens the route by almost 45km.

If you are making use of the West Coast Train Line and have travelled to Carlisle from the south of England, head to Penrith Railway Station on NCN 71 to finish. This shortens your journey by 10km and takes 1.5hrs off the travelling time including connections. Don't forget to book your bike onto the train in advance.

Schedules

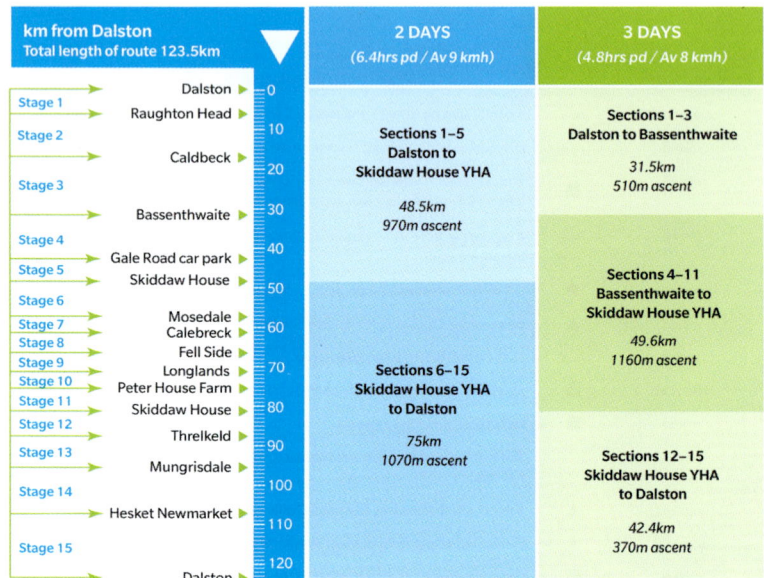

Directions

1 Exit Dalston Station on a cut-through to Barras Lane. Turn ←. Continue to Carlisle Rd, then turn →, fork ← for the NCN 10 and follow this to Bridge End. Continue past **Bridge End Inn** as the road climbs gently round a corner. Shortly turn onto a paved road on your left signed the Cumbria Way. This is also off-road NCN 10 (aka Reivers Off-road Route). Head south, past Hawksdale Hall and Holmhill Farm, until you reach Lime House School. Here split with the Cumbria Way and bear ← through a wood and over a bridge. Take a → and continue on NCN 10 until you reach the main road once more. Turn ← and continue to **Raughton Head**.

2 With the church on your left, turn → before the stone memorial. Now follow NCN 7 through a farm yard towards Thethwaite. Turn → and, after 600 metres, → again at a junction signed Bell Bridge ½ Welton 1½. Before Bell Bridge, take the bridleway on your left signed St Mary's Church. Follow the car-wide track as it heads uphill. After the church turn → and continue to a

Route 6 – Dalston/Skiddaw Mega Pretzel

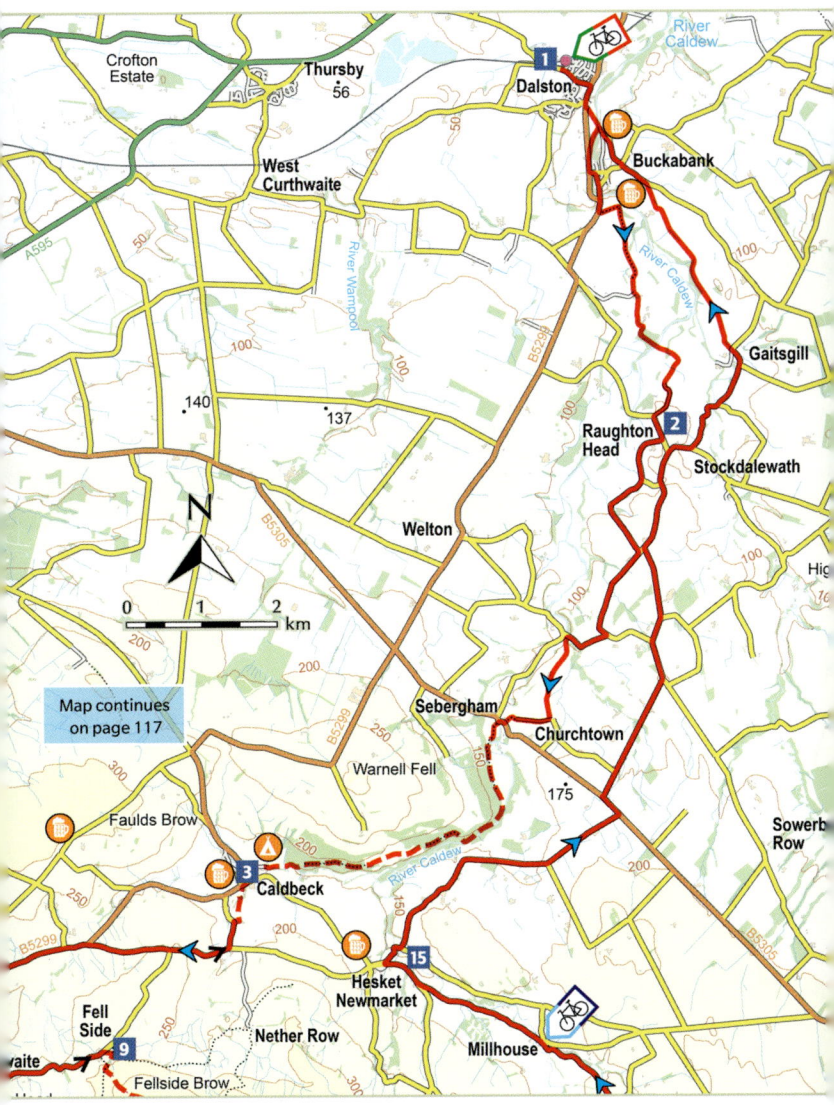

Into Parson's Park close to Caldbeck

road, then turn → and head over the bridge. Immediately after the bridge, follow signs for the Cumbria Way on the left and continue south as it follows the River Caldew through Parson's Park to **Caldbeck**.

3 ■ On meeting the main road turn ← over the bridge and bear →. Continue ↑ past the Oddfellows Arms on your left. Continue out of town uphill. Fork ← by Fellview Primary School and head through Townhead, bearing → onto Smithy Ln. Reach a T-junction. Turn → onto The Street signed Fellside Uldale/NCN 10 (Reivers). On meeting the B5299 continue ↑. Cross a small river followed by a cattle grid and begin to climb onto open land. Follow the NCN 10 to **Uldale**. With the Snooty Fox Country Inn on your right continue through the village and continue taking signs for Keswick. After a small rise the landscape opens up, and a concrete drive on your left signals the start of a bridleway. Follow this to the road and head to **Bassenthwaite**.

4 When you meet the road turn ← and shortly bear ← again before heading over a bridge. Continue past The Sun Inn until you reach a junction opposite a farm. Turn ← and then fork → onto School Road. Continue south at the crossroads through the village of Chapel Bridge for 2km until you reach a junction, then turn ← and continue on a tree-lined road towards the hill.

Route 6 – Dalston/Skiddaw Mega Pretzel

When you reach the **A591** turn → and follow signs for Keswick. After 3km take a ← signposted Skiddaw and leave the main road behind and begin to climb, first through **Millbeck** and then on to **Applethwaite**. Continue bearing ← and then fork ← by Applethwaite Country House onto Gale Road. Continue climbing through the woods until the road runs out and you reach a **car park**.

5 ● Head through the gate at the far end of the car park. Turn ←, signposted the Cumbria Way and Skiddaw House. Follow the track as it hugs the shoulder of **Lonscale Fell**. After 2km of technical single-track and stunning views, the landscape opens up. Maintain your course to **Skiddaw House YHA**.

> **Skiddaw House YHA** features twice on this route. It's a unique location with a lovely atmosphere and is worth an overnight stop either for a bed or to camp (book in advance, and as it's offline it's cash only). Food can be brought and prepared in the simple kitchen. There are logs for the fire and a drying rack!
>
> It has operated as a YHA since 1987 and hopefully will continue to open its doors to tired walkers and riders. However, at the time of writing it is on the market. It is hard to imagine it as anything other than a YHA due to its unique position perched within this very exposed landscape, but it is worth making inquiries in advance should you decide to break up your journey there.

6 ▲ Now follow the Cumbria Way as it forks east along the Caldew Valley. When the single-track becomes a good, car-wide track, continue over a bridge and take the → fork towards Swineside. From here it's 2km of road to **Mosedale**.

7 Turn ← at the junction and follow the hedgeless road as it hugs the eastern side of the massif for 4km until you reach **Calebreck**.

8 ■ Take the car-wide track on the left signposted 'bridleway Fellside 3 miles'. Climb out over open fells before descending. Turn → and continue to the farmyard at **Fell Side**.

9 ■ Follow the NCN 10 through **Branthwaite** to **Green Head**. Here the NCN 10 (Reivers Off-road Route) leads you over the shoulder of White Hill and delivers a fast descent and great views before dropping you down to **Longlands**.

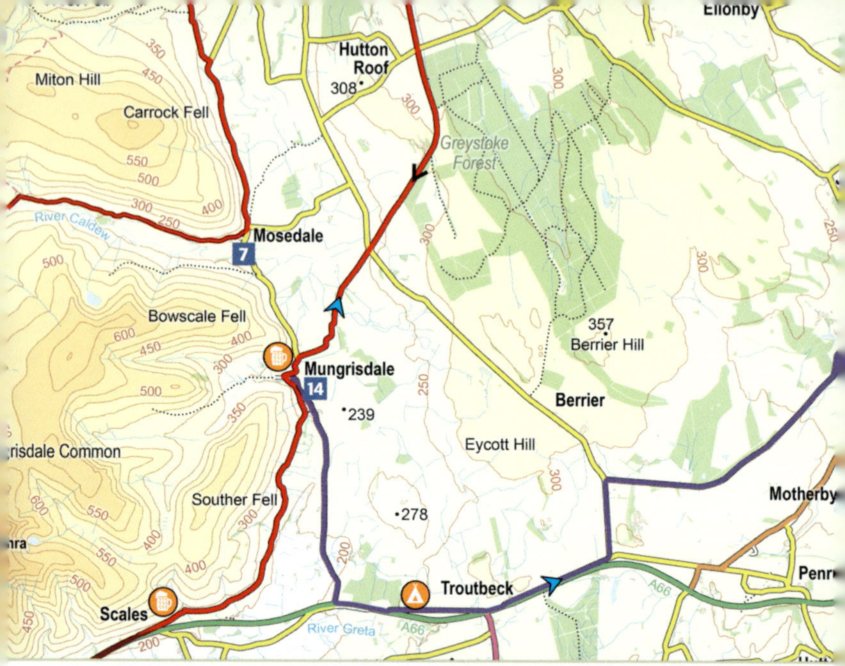

Dash Falls beside the track to Skiddaw

10 Turn ← and, ignoring the right signed NCN 10 after 1km, continue along the Cumbria Way as it follows the road. Maintain your direction until **Peter House Farm**.

11 ▲ Turn ← and the Cumbria Way now leads you back onto Skiddaw on a good car-wide asphalt driveway. After 1km take a rough car-wide track to the right. In the distance Dash Falls can be seen. Climb the steep track with the falls on your left. Head through the gate and the track begins to level out. After a further kilometre Skiddaw House becomes visible in the distance. The Skiddaw House YHA has an 'honesty café' for basic refreshments and water. Be sure to bring cash.

12 ▲ The path leads to the gate of **Skiddaw House YHA**. Head south initially on the same part of the Cumbria Way you followed when you first came past Skiddaw House 32.5km earlier. After 1.2km take a sharp ← and descend bearing → as the single-track heads around the shoulder of Blease Fell, delivering a stunning descent all the way to the road and **Threlkeld** beyond.

119

Tough, technical single-track on the southern access to Skiddaw

13 ■ On reaching the town fork ← and then fork ← again onto the NCN 71. After a short climb, reach the **A66**. Continue parallel to the busy road on a cycle path for 1km before taking the ← fork at Scales Farm. Continue around the shoulder of **Souther Fell** until **Mungrisdale**.

14 After Mungrisdale, continue north and take the next → signposted Hutton Roof 2½. Continue until a T-junction signposted Calebreck 3, Penrith 12. Turn ←. After 100 metres turn →, signposted Millhouse, and maintain your direction to **Hesket Newmarket**.

15 On reaching the town centre, fork sharply → and rejoin the NCN 10. Head through Newlands. Continue as the road bears first → then ← until you meet a junction. Turn ← following the sign for the NCN (Reivers). After 200 metres, beyond the Sour Nook Inn, take a → turn, sticking with the NCN 10. Climb steadily and bear ← when the road forks. After 300 metres leave the NCN 10, ignoring the left fork and instead bear → signposted Raughton Head, High Bridge, Carlisle. Continue on this road, ignoring forks to the right and left, until you reach **Raughton Head**. Now take the ← signposted Welton, Dalston, Carlisle. Follow the road as it bears ←, ignoring the NCN 10 route signs. Cross a long narrow stone bridge. Bear → as the road follows the NCN 7 back to **Dalston**.

Route 6 – Dalston/Skiddaw Mega Pretzel

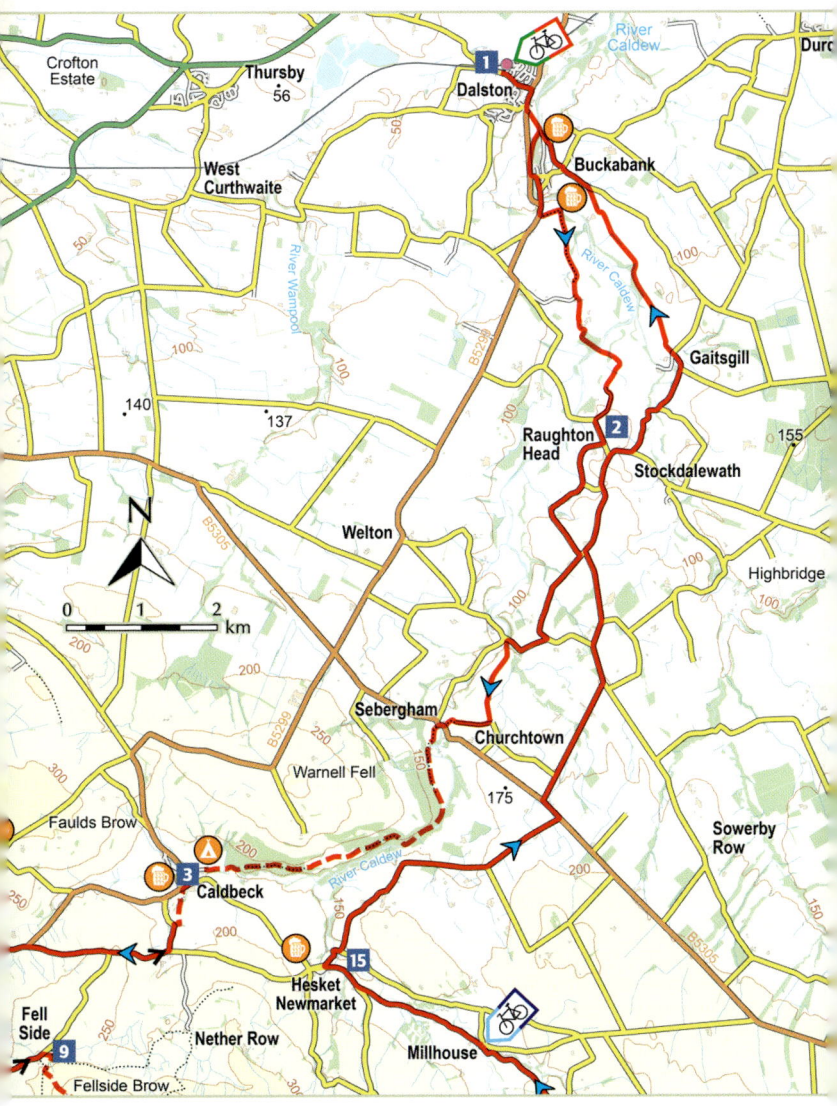

7 — 55% off road

Route 7
Penrith/High Street Circuit

Start/finish	Penrith Railway Station
Total distance	84km (52 miles)
Off-road distance	46km
Percentage off-road	55%
Total ascent/descent	2060m
Grade	Hard ●
Time	2–3 days
Terrain	Single-track 21%, track 34%, road 45%
Bike choice	Gravel/MTB

Introduction

The Far Eastern Fells are wild and exposed. The rural villages and sheep farms seem more focused on the immediate tasks at hand than their more quaint neighbours to the west. The first day is a series of short, tough climbs over the shoulders of fells, while day two takes on one of the most challenging climbs in the Lakes. There are limited opportunities to buy provisions after leaving Penrith so take supplies.

Overview

The route begins in the friendly and picturesque market town of Penrith in the far north eastern corner of the Lake District. Journey south along minor roads on the far eastern flank of the Lake District as the high fells of the route's main objective, High Street, dominate the skyline to your right. The first challenge begins on the Old Corpse Road over Swindale Common. From there follow a short section along the edge of Haweswater Reservoir to the foot of a tough climb up to Gatesgarth Pass. The descent is one of the finest in the Lakes. Next, follow an old pack-road over the fell to Kentmere before a further pull uphill passes close to Troutbeck. From here it's a long steady climb up to High Street and the Straits of Riggindale before a high-altitude traverse leads down The Pen and back to Helton and on to Penrith to the north.

Heading off-route and into Shap for food

Bikepacking in the Lake District

Summary table

Waypoint	Section	Distance (km)	Ascent (m)	Descent (m)
1	Penrith Railway Station – Askham	8.7	90	50
2	Askham – Mardale Head	18.7	410	360
3	Mardale Head – Sadgill	6.3	310	380
4	Sadgill – Kentmere	4.1	130	190
5	Kentmere – Troutbeck	11.7	210	160
6	Troutbeck – High Street	8.7	635	80
7	High Street – Askham	17.2	220	730
8	Askham – Penrith	8.6	55	110

Schedules

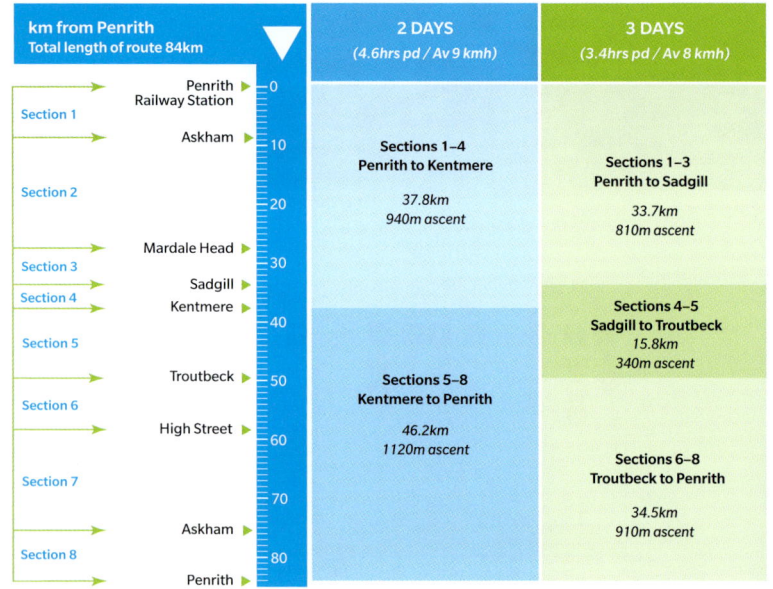

Route 7 – Penrith/High Street Circuit

Surface	Grade	Description
paved	n/a	After leaving the town, head towards the foothills
mixed	●	Leafy lanes lead you to the Old Corpse Road
unpaved	●	Some managable hike-a-bike rewards you with a classic Lakeland descent
unpaved	●	Tough pack-road
mixed	▲	Undulating country roads and enjoyable off-road descent
unpaved	●	A long pull to an ancient Roman road
unpaved	▲	High-level descent in a rarefied wilderness
paved	n/a	Country lanes return you to the welcoming market town

Alternative start/finish suggestions

The standard start/finish for this route is Penrith Railway Station. If you are journeying to the start by car consider starting the ride at Askham, shortening the route by 17.5km. If arriving from the south you could consider starting and ending the route at Windermere Railway Station, 2km south of the route's southern apex (close to Stage 6), and heading south on reaching Askham. This would not shorten travelling time, due to connections, but would take 14km off the route. If approaching from the west a start could be made at Hartsop where you would gain the route via a section of the Lakeland 200.

Directions

1 With your back to the station turn ←. At the roundabout take the first exit on the left and bear → as the road levels out before descending. At the junction take a → onto Penrith High Street and continue south on this, through the town centre. Cross the roundabout using the pedestrian crossing. The road descends into **Eamont Bridge**. Head over the river and take the first → at a junction flanked by two pubs. Cross the M6 motorway and descend into **Yanwath**. Bear ← and climb gently, following the road to the picturesque village of **Askham**.

Bikepacking in the Lake District

2 ● Continue through Askham and fork ←, signposted Whale/Knipe. At the first junction turn ← towards Bampton Grange. Bampton has a post office and there is a Co-op at Shap, 4km off-route to the east. At **Bampton Grange** turn → and then cross the bridge and bear ← through Bomby Farm. At Toathmain fork → and follow this road to Swindale Lane and continue to Swindale Head. Take the bridleway on the right, signed Old Corpse Road. This climbs steeply before bearing ← and levelling out. Continue for 1km before descending steeply to a minor road flanking **Haweswater Reservoir**. Turn ← and follow the road to a car park at **Mardale Head**. The following climb is mainly hike-a-bike but is justified by the pay off: one of the finest classic MTB descents in the Lakes.

3 ● When the road runs out beyond the car park take the bridleway on the left. This is rideable at first but steepens rapidly. You will have to push or carry your bike to the pass. After topping out at **Gatesgarth Pass** you can descend on a rough car-wide track to a stone bridge and a gate at Brownhowe Bottom. Once you are through the gate it's unbroken pack-road until the valley floor.

Gatesgarth Pass: one of the best descents in the Lakes

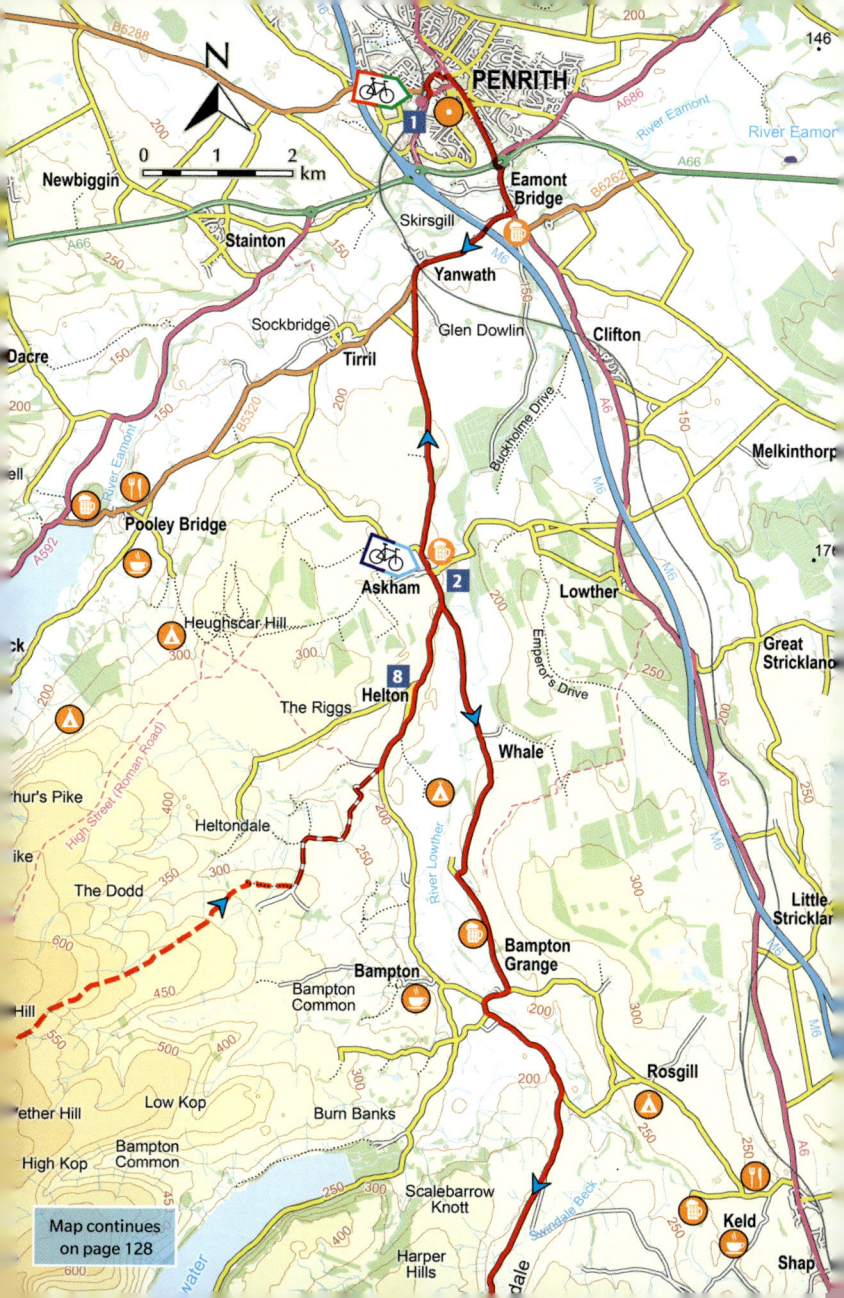

Bikepacking in the Lake District

4 ● When the asphalt starts at **Sadgill**, turn immediately → and head over the bridge. Take the bridleway on the left, first on road and then car-wide track. After ascending steeply the pack-road bears round to the → as it cuts over the fell. A welcome descent delivers you back to a minor road where you turn ← and head south. After 800 metres, descend on a sharp → and bear ←. Turn → over the bridge and head into **Kentmere**.

5 ▲ Bear ← and follow a bridleway, signposted below the church. At Kentmere Hall bear ← and follow the bridleway, with the wood on your left, as it ascends onto open ground. Bear → as it hugs the shoulder of Whiteside End. Ignore the left fork and continue until the bridleway reaches a T-junction. Turn → and bear ←. Before reaching High House, turn → towards High Borrans. Follow the bridleway as it bears ← onto Borans Lane. When this reaches a road turn → and progress 600 metres before forking onto a bridleway, **Dubbs Road**. After 1.5km take the sharp ← fork and then after descending 400 metres, a sharp → fork. At Troutbeck, 1km off the route, there is a pub and a few places to stay including Windermere YHA (book in advance) but few amenities.

Windermere YHA

Route 7 – Penrith/High Street Circuit

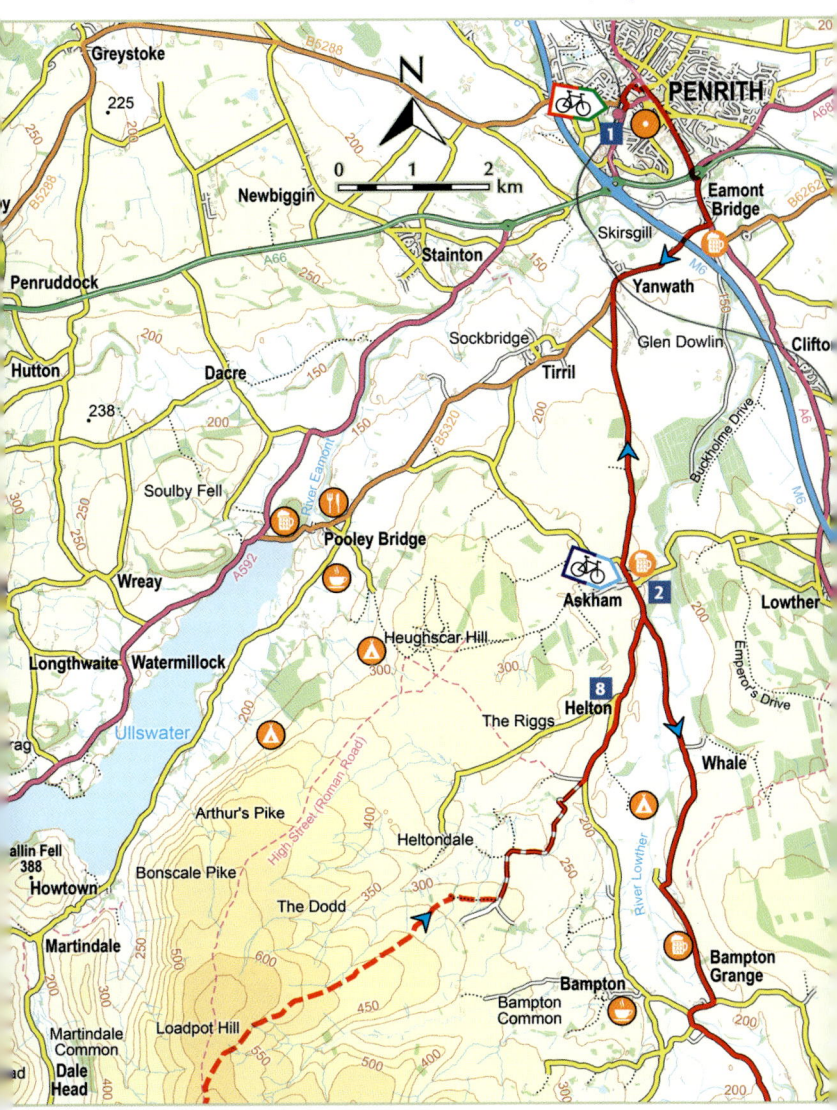

High Street: the ancient Roman road between Penrith and Ambleside

Racecourse Hill

Route 7 – Penrith/High Street Circuit

6 ● The following climb to High Street rises 600 metres over 7km. The climb is gradual for the first 4km. When you reach Park Fell, the bridleway heads steeply upwards with Wander Scar on your right until you reach **High Street**, the remains of a lonely, exposed Roman road linking Penrith and Ambleside. With Thornthwaite Crag in sight to your left, fork → towards the High Street Fell and Racecourse Hill – the highest point of the route at 828m.

7 ▲ The bridleway descends ←, adjacent to the low stone wall. As you climb again along the Straits of Riggindale take a → fork towards Kidsty Pike. The basin of Riggindale dominates the view to your right. Before the pike, bear ← towards High Raise. As you descend north the going is mainly rideable but is often broken and boggy. Before you reach **Loadpot Hill** fork → on a bridleway that descends gradually before arriving at a track that progresses to a road. Turn ← and follow it to **Heltondale**, over the cattle grid. Fork ← and take signs for Helton.

8 From **Helton** continue to **Askham**. Head through the town and fork → taking signs for Penrith. At **Yanwath** bear → and cross the railway tracks and continue over the M6. Turn ← onto the A6 and continue through **Eamont Bridge**. Cross the roundabout via the pedestrian walkway. Head into **Penrith**. Bear ← for the railway station.

8   22% off road

Route 8
Nine Lakes

Start/finish	Windermere Railway Station
Total distance	254.7km (158¼ miles)
Off-road distance	53km
Percentage off-road	22%
Total ascent/descent	4590m
Grade	Very hard ◆
Time	3–5 days
Terrain	Single-track 11%, track 11%, road 78%
Bike choice	Gravel/MTB

Introduction

Anyone familiar with the Lake District knows it to be a mountainous place, a series of fells and accompanying lakes that fan round 360 degrees like petals on a flower. With the exception of the Lakeland 200, the majority of routes in this guide focus on one area and provide a two- or three-day circular route that allows the rider to explore the wildest and inaccessible trails on offer there. This often involves high off-road passes, sections of hike-a-bike and difficult terrain at the mercy of the elements. This route is designed to offer something different. Like the Lakeland 200, this route circumnavigates the Lakes, but this one aims to introduce the rider to many classic road passes and lake-side vistas. Sections of high-level bridleway are included to link you to the next valley. There are great rewards, and while less than 25km of this route overlaps with the Lakeland 200, be warned: this is a long route. Set aside three or four days depending on the time of year.

Wasdale Fell

Overview

Setting out from Windermere Railway Station, take a direct route to Ambleside along the A591. Now follow the off-road national cycle network (NCN) 6 down Lake Windemere's western shore before taking minor roads to Newby Bridge. Pick your way round the Furness Fells on tranquil lanes and pick up a national cycle path following the eastern banks of Coniston Water. After Coniston, follow the NCN 637 to Little Langdale. Now take the road climb up to Wrynose Pass, shortly followed by the famous Hardknott Pass, before continuing down the Esk Valley until Eskdale Green, then take a bridleway through Miterdale Forest to Nether Wasdale. Head north east along the northern shore of Wast Water and on to Wasdale Head. Here, head north on a bridleway over the infamous Black Sail Pass before continuing along forestry track beside Ennerdale Water. On joining the road, follow NCN 71 to Loweswater and continue to Buttermere. From here climb the Newlands Pass before descending into Keswick. Head south until the road runs out then ascend Watendale Fell and continue over to Thirlmere Reservoir. Follow the road north until joining the Old Coach Road that cuts across the north of Matterdale. When this reaches Ullswater continue south and skirt the shore to Glenridding before crossing Patterdale and, joining a spectacular bridleway, following the lake shore into Sandwick. Remain on minor roads to Pooley Bridge before heading south again to Askham and on to Haweswater and the final challenge: Gatesgarth Pass. The final road section back to Windermere is well deserved.

Bikepacking in the Lake District

Summary table

Waypoint	Section	Distance (km)	Ascent (m)	Descent (m)
1	Windermere – Newby Bridge	29.5	300	380
2	Newby Bridge – Coniston	25.0	370	360
3	Coniston – Wrynose Pass	9.8	430	100
4	Wrynose Pass – Wasdale Head	30.5	400	710
5	Wasdale Head – Black Sail Hut	5.0	450	250
6	Black Sail Hut – Buttermere	33.0	360	520
7	Buttermere – Keswick	13.9	250	300
8	Keswick – Thirlmere Reservoir	15.4	500	370
9	Thirlmere Reservoir – Patterdale	29.0	500	550
10	Patterdale – Pooley Bridge	15.0	220	220
11	Pooley Bridge – Mardale Head	21.2	310	200
12	Mardale Head – Garnett Bridge	14.2	330	470
13	Garnett Bridge – Windermere	13.2	170	160

Alternative start/finish suggestions

Windermere has been chosen for the start of this route as it is synonymous with Lakeland and provides instant access to stunning views. However, there are alternative start/finish locations that could prove convenient or offer

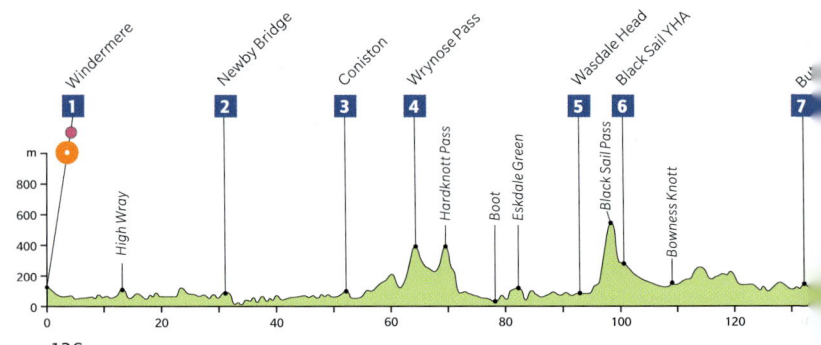

Route 8 – Nine Lakes

Surface	Grade	Description
mixed	🟩	A fast start followed by a tranquil, lake-side introduction to the route
paved	n/a	Wooded climbing followed by a gentle lake-side traverse with the Old Man of Coniston in view
mixed	🟩	Low-level wooded single-track is abruptly ended by a savage 1-in-3 climb to a remote valley
paved	n/a	A second brutal climb to Hardknott Pass is followed by a fast descent into Eskdale before the route takes you east again to Wasdale
unpaved	◆	Tough hike-a-bike in remote surroundings offering exceptional views
mixed	🟩	10km of descent along forestry roads takes you back to the NCN 71 before you roll past Crummock Water to Buttermere
paved	n/a	Climb the famous Newlands Pass and then descend for 15km into Keswick
mixed	🔴	After reaching an isolated valley, strike out on an indistinct bridleway past a lonely tarn to secluded plantation with great wild camping options
mixed	🔺	The picturesque roads flanking the reservoir lead to a long haul on the Old Coach Road to Ullswater
mixed	🔺	Refuel here before beginning the narrow single-track that skirts the lake
paved	n/a	Easy going introduction to the Far Eastern Fells
mixed	🔴	The famous Gatesgarth Pass is followed by the stunning Longsleddale
paved	n/a	The final warm-down as you roll through wooded lanes to Staveley and Windermere beyond

alternative perspectives. If you are coming from the north by train consider starting at Askham or Pooley Bridge near Penrith. Keswick could also provide a suitable starting point.

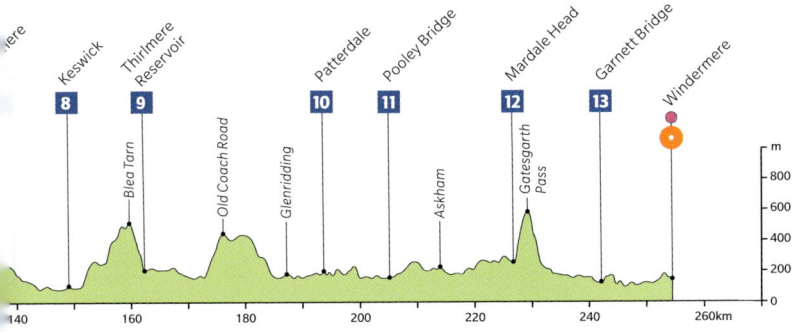

Schedules

km from Windermere
Total length of route 254.7km

Location	km
Windermere Railway Station	0
Section 1	
Newby Bridge	30
Section 2	
Coniston	55
Section 3	
Wrynose Pass	65
Section 4	
Wasdale Head	95
Black Sail YHA	100
Section 6	
Buttermere	135
Section 7	
Keswick	145
Section 8	
Thirlmere Reservoir	160
Section 9	
Patterdale	190
Section 10	
Pooley Bridge	205
Section 11	
Mardale Head	225
Section 12	
Garnet Bridge	240
Section 13	
Windermere Railway Station	254.7

2 DAYS (12.7hrs pd / Av 10 kph)

Sections 1–6
Windermere to Buttermere
132.8km
2310m ascent

Sections 7–13
Buttermere to Windermere
121.9km
2280m ascent

3 DAYS (9.4hrs pd / Av 9 kph)

Sections 1–4
Windermere to Wasdale Head
94.8km
1500m ascent

Sections 5–8
Wasdale Head to Thirlmere Reservoir
67.3km
1560m ascent

Sections 9–13
Thirlmere Reservoir to Windermere
92.6km
1530m ascent

4 DAYS (7.9hrs pd / Av 8 kph)

Sections 1–2
Windermere to Coniston
54.5km
670m ascent

Sections 3–5
Coniston to Black Sail YHA
45.3km
1280m ascent

Sections 6–8
Black Sail YHA to Thirlmere Reservoir
62.3km
1110m ascent

Sections 9–13
Thirlmere Reservoir to Windermere
92.6km
1530m ascent

5 DAYS (7.2hrs pd / Av 7 kph)

Sections 1–2
Windermere to Coniston
54.5km
670m ascent

Sections 3–5
Coniston to Black Sail YHA
45.3km
1280m ascent

Sections 6–8
Black Sail YHA to Thirlmere Reservoir
62.3km
1110m ascent

Sections 9–11
Thirlmere Reservoir to Mardale Head
65.2km
1030m ascent

Sections 12–13
Mardale Head to Windermere
27.4km
500m ascent

Route 8 – Nine Lakes

Directions

1 ■ Leave Windermere Railway Station and head north on the A591. At Waterhead (on the outskirts of Ambleside), bear ← onto the A5075. Take a ← signed Hawkshead/Coniston. Follow the road over Rothay Bridge onto the A593. Fork ← over a bridge towards Clappersgate before a ← onto the undulating B5286. After a short rise turn ←. Just beyond the gatehouse to Wray Castle, take a ←. Continue on the bridleway along the edge of the lake, past the ferry access road on your left. Follow the road before forking ← and continuing to High Cunsey and through Hammer Hole. At the next junction fork ←. Follow the road through **Lakeside** and continue to **Newby Bridge**.

2 Just before the Swan Hotel, fork → signed Haverthwaite. Continue past the weir and over the railway bridge. At the four-way junction take the second ← and continue through **Bouth** towards Spark Bridge. Turn → before the bridge and follow the road towards Lowick Bridge. Before the bridge in **Lowick Bridge**, fork → and head along Crake Valley. At Arklid Farm take the → signed 'Coniston via east of lake 10 miles'. Maintain your course before forking ← and continuing around the head of **Coniston Water** towards the town.

The Old Man of Coniston beyond the lake

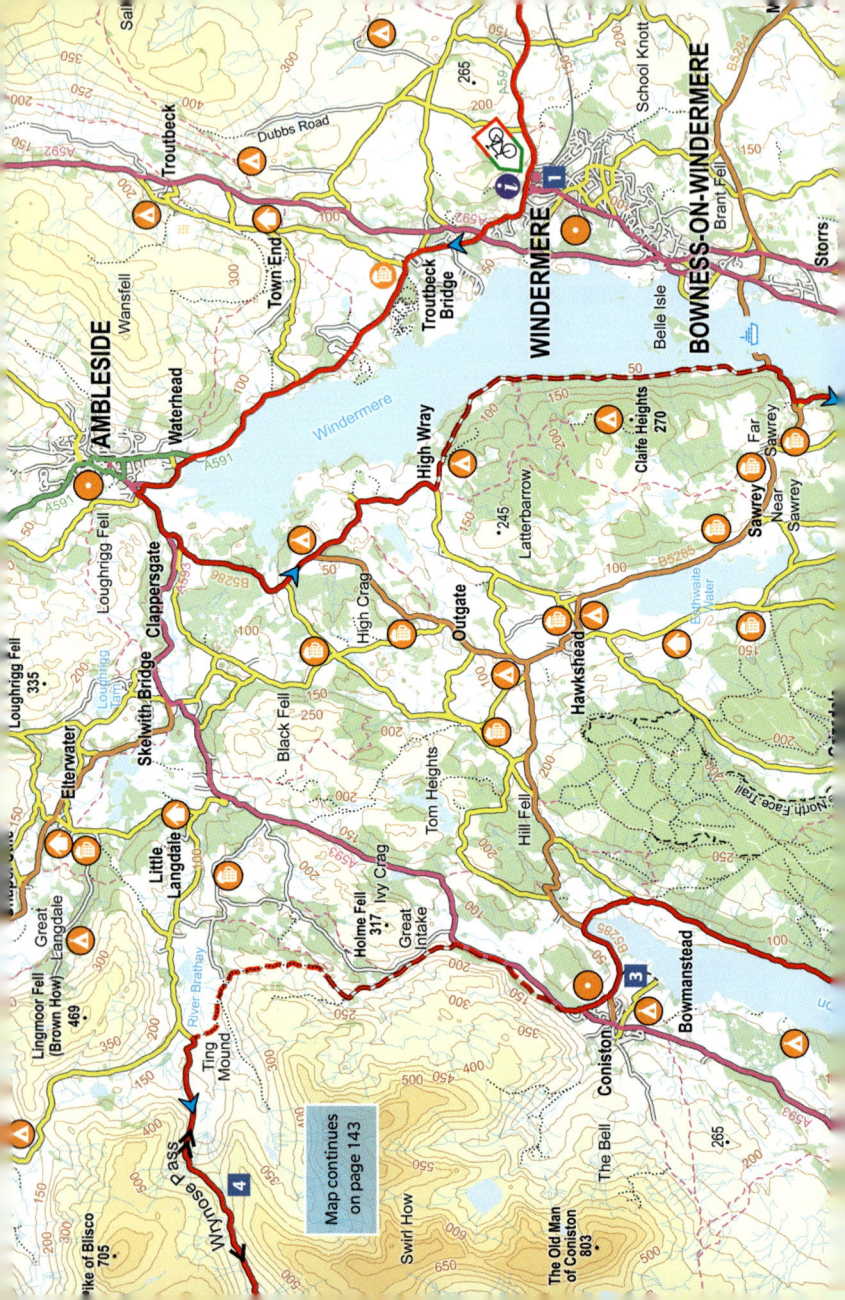

Route 8 – Nine Lakes

3 ■ Before reaching the centre of **Coniston**, fork → and follow the road until a bridleway on your left takes you onto a gravel path running adjacent with the road. Follow this until it rejoins the road and then at **Great Intake**, take the ← fork onto a minor road. Follow the road until it runs out then fork ← onto a bridleway. Follow this through woods and bear ← until Bridge End. Cross two bridges and fork ←.

> **Wrynose** and **Hardknott** passes are classic Lakeland road climbs. The tight switchbacks are hard work when you are carrying your luggage and trying to keep the front wheel on the road!

4 Follow the thin hedgeless road as it snakes over **Wrynose Pass** and then descend along Wrynose Bottom. After forking → over Cockley Beck Bridge climb to **Hardknott Pass**. Descend along Eskdale through **Boot** and past Dalegarth Station. Follow the road through the village of **Eskdale Green** and fork → after The Bowerhouse Inn. Continue to **Santon Bridge**. Here fork →

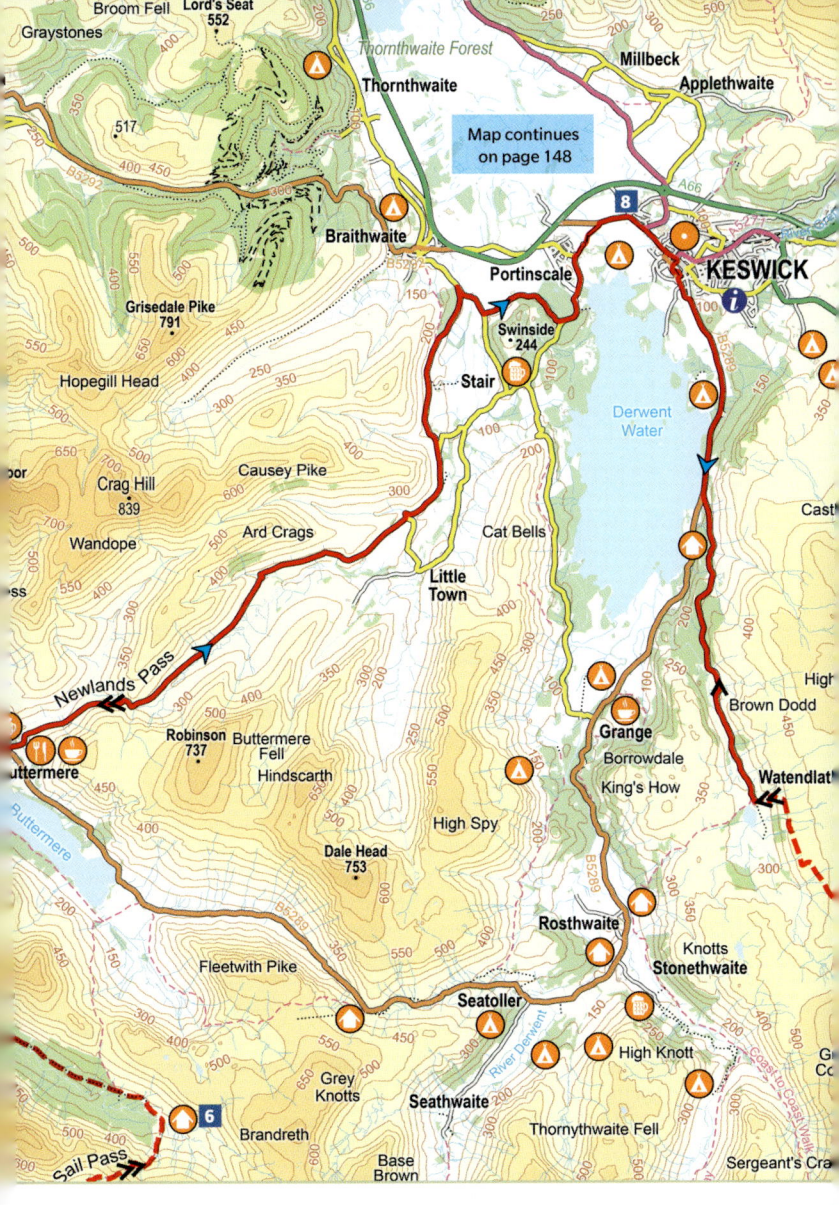

Bikepacking in the Lake District

for Nether Wasdale. Before reaching the village, follow the → fork towards Wasdale and continue along the west shore of **Wast Water** to **Wasdale Head**.

> This route keeps you on asphalt and gravel where possible but the **Black Sail Pass** hike-a-bike is unavoidable and is the lesser of two evils. The alternative bridleway to Seatoller via Seathwaite is harder and badly defined, and rewards you with an extra-long climb up Honister Pass and then over Scarth Gap before you can reach the Ennerdale Valley.

5 ◆ Behind and to the right of the Wasdale Inn, your bridleway follows the beck. Take the ← fork. The rideable path soon runs out. Push, pull, haul and carry your bike up the western flank of **Kirk Fell**, over a beck and on to the pass. This takes between 1.5 and 2 hr. From the pass drop → and follow a stream until it delivers you to the secluded Ennerdale Valley and the **Black Sail YHA**.

6 ■ With the YHA on your right follow a car-wide track through a gate and along the valley as it snakes through the forest. Continue with Ennerdale Water on your left as the road bears → below **Bowness Knott** before bearing ← to **Croasdale**. Take the → over Croasdale Bridge and climb gently on a minor road that hugs the edge of the park border. Follow signs for NCN 71 through **Lamplaugh** and on to Fangs Brow Farm. Fork →, signed Loweswater. Ignore the left signed NCN 71 and continue past **Loweswater** over Scalehill Bridge. Continue until you take a sharp → fork, signed Buttermere 4, and descend to the shore of Crummock Water. Follow the road into **Buttermere**.

7 On reaching Buttermere head past the hotel and over the bridge, then climb for 100 metres before taking a ← signed Keswick 8½. It's a hard slog up to **Newlands Pass** but a fantastic descent along Keskadale Beck Valley. Ignore two right turns before taking a sharp → fork, signed Swindale 1, returns you to the NCN 71. Continue until a ← fork signed Ullock ¼. The minor road merges with a busier one; follow the signs for Keswick. On reaching **Portinscale** village on a left-hand bend, take a → signed Derwentwater Hotel. Follow the road until you reach a footbridge. Dismount and cross the bridge. Continue on a quiet road until you meet the busy B5289 then turn →.

> This next section is tough. You will be taking a **bridleway across an open fell** that allows you to avoid the A591 and ride a stunning section of NCN 6 along the banks of Thirlmere Reservoir with views of the mighty Helvellyn. You could choose to exclude this fell from the route and ride from Keswick to St John's in the Vale.

Route 8 – Nine Lakes

8 ● Bear → on the B5289, then head over the bridge and continue towards the centre of **Keswick**. At the mini-roundabout take the third exit (your direction →) and follow the road round to the ← on Heads Road. Continue south on the busy Borrowdale Road until you take the first minor road on your left, signed Ashness Br. Watendlath. Climb steeply through Ashness Wood with **Derwent Water** to your right. Continue into the secluded valley with Watendale Beck on your right until you reach the car park at **Watendlath**. The bridleway starts left of the carpark and heads up the steep, ancient steps of a pack-road. After 200 metres take the → fork over a stream while the footpath continues upwards. Head towards **Blea Tarn** on an open fell and a badly defined bridleway. Beyond the tarn, climb towards the pass between two boulders in front of you to the left. From there head downhill into the forest. Pick your way through the trees on a good path until you reach the magical Harrop Tarn. The banks of the tarn would be an excellent spot for a peaceful wild camp. Cross a wooden bridge and immediately pick out an indistinct path on your left that you now need to descend on to reach the road. The rocks can be slippery so take care. On reaching the road on the west bank of **Thirlmere** head through a small gate and turn ←.

A rough, tricky descent from Harrop Tarn down to Thirlmere

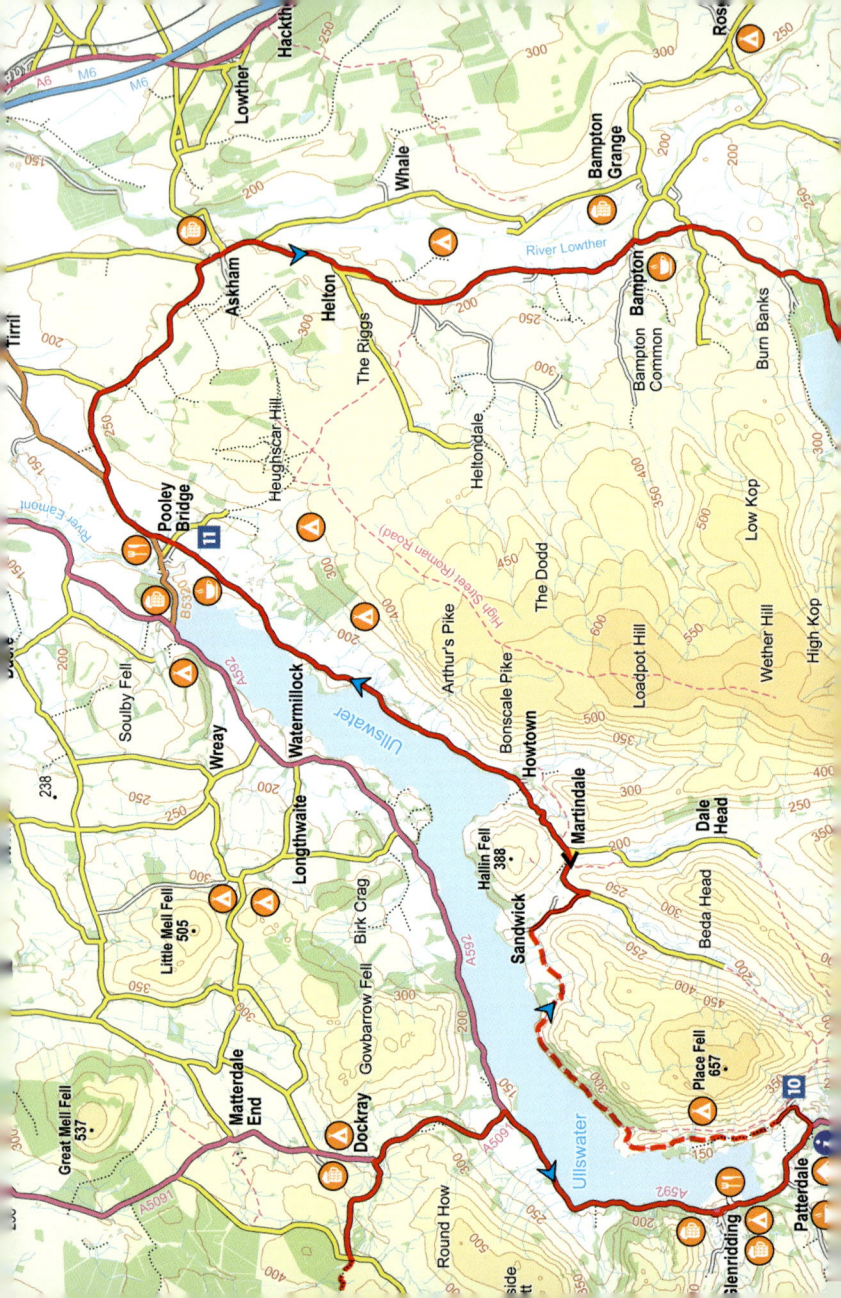

Bikepacking in the Lake District

9 ▲ Follow the road along the edge of the water before forking → past a car park and continuing along the dam of the reservoir as the road bears ←. Head over the `A591` onto a minor road signed 'Keswick by bike'. This short section of car-wide track delivers you to the `B5322`. Turn ← and continue north to **St John's in the Vale** on the NCN 6. Immediately after a farm on your right look out for a NCN 71 sign and turn → signed Matterdale (unsuitable for vehicles). Follow the **Old Coach Road** as it snakes over the shoulder of Matterdale Common for the next 7km to High Row. Drop into **Dockray** then turn → when you meet the `A5091`. Follow this to **Ullswater** and at the T-junction turn → onto the `A592` and continue to **Glenridding**. The R&R Cornershop at Glenridding is a great spot to refuel. Continue on the `A592` over a bridge and through **Patterdale**. On a right-hand bend take a ← marked as a dead end with restricted vehicle width. Continue over a long narrow bridge and follow the road until it runs out and a gate provides access to a bridleway.

10 ▲ Take the lower of the two bridleways on offer here when you reach the gate and continue ↑ through Side Farm and head north. There's a lovely looking campsite on the east shore of Ullswater at Side Farm that could be a good place to rest. Continue along the rocky undulating bridleway through the forests that cover Ullswater's shore on Birk Fell and maintain your direction towards **Sandwick**. Fork → when you rejoin the road and take a sharp ← at the junction towards Howtown. It's a steep climb over the Coombs to St Peter's Church followed by a steeper descent to **Howtown**. Skirt past the village and maintain your route all the way to the outskirts of **Pooley Bridge**.

11 At the crossroads east of Pooley Bridge continue ↑ and meet up with the `B5320`. Take the first → onto a minor road that snakes round the northern shoulder of Heughscar Hill. Head through **Askham** and on to **Helton**. When you reach **Bampton** turn → over the bridge and continue taking signs for Haweswater. Head over Naddle Bridge and bear ← on a minor road that skirts the edge of **Haweswater Reservoir**. Continue to the car park at **Mardale Head**.

12 ● When the road runs out, head through a gate at the end of the car park. Ignore routes to your right and continue ↑ on a rough car-wide bridleway signed for Gatesgarth Pass. Rideable track gives way to rough hike-a-bike but it's all well-defined and the pass is in sight above you. The climb to the pass takes around one hour. Once you top out it becomes rideable once more.

Route 8 – Nine Lakes

Nearly done...at 200km!

Descend steeply to Brownhowe Bottom, over a stone bridge and through the gate. Now enjoy the views during the spectacular descent down a rough pack-road to **Longsleddale**. Once you are back on tarmac, continue south to the head of the valley at **Garnett Bridge**.

13 Cross Garnett Bridge and bear → before taking a → onto Potter Fell Road. At the next junction take a → and continue to **Staveley**. Turn ← over the bridge and ← again onto Kentmere Road before turning → at the war memorial. Head to the A591 and join a cycle path that runs along the side of the road. At **Ings** follow signs for NCR 6 as it crosses the busy A road and continues to Windermere. As you drop into **Windermere** look out for signs for the train station on your left.

Appendix A
Lake District campsites and hostels

Route 1 – The Lakeland 200

Staveley to Ambleside

Windermere Camping and Caravanning Club Site (3km off-route)
Ashes Ln
Staveley
Kendal
LA8 9JS
tel 01539 821119
www.campingandcaravanningclub.co.uk

Pound Farm Caravan Park (3km off-route)
Crook
Kendal
LA8 8JZ
tel 01539 821220
www.poundfarmleisurepark.co.uk

Ings Kippers Campsite and Shepherds Hut (2km off-route)
Hill TopIngs
Kendal
LA8 9PY
tel 07306 410391
www.pitchup.com

Kentmere Farm Pods
Browfoot Farm
Brow Foot Ln
Kendal
LA8 9JQ
tel 01539 821210
www.farmpods.co.uk

High Borrans Lodges
Windermere
LA23 1JS
tel 015394 43313
www.windermere-lodge.com

Troutbeck Camping Pods
Poole Bank Farm
Troutbeck
Windermere
LA23 1PN
tel 07891 634592

YHA Ambleside Hostel
Waterhead
Ambleside
LA22 0EU
tel 0345 371 9620
www.yha.org.uk/hostel/yha-ambleside

Ambleside to Coniston

Baysbrown Farm Campsite
Great Langdale
Ambleside
LA22 9JZ
tel 015394 37150
www.baysbrownfarmcampsite.co.uk

Low Wray Campsite
Low Wray
Ambleside
LA22 0JA
tel 015394 32733
www.nationaltrust.org.uk

Appendix A – Lake District campsites and hostels

4 Winds Lakeland Tipis (2km off-route)
Low Wray
Ambleside
LA22 0JA
www.glamping-uk.co.uk

Hawkshead Hall Campsite
(2km off-route)
Hawkshead
Ambleside
LA22 0NN
tel 015394 36221
www.yha.org.uk/hostel/yha-hawkshead

Grizedale Campsite (5km off-route)
Bowkerstead Farm
Satterthwaite
Ulverston
LA12 8LL
tel 01229 860208
www.grizedale-camping.co.uk

The Croft Caravan Site (2km off-route)
Croft Meadow House
Hawkshead
Ambleside
LA22 0NX
tel 015394 36374
www.hawksheadcroft.co.uk

Abbot Park Farm Campsite
(7km off-route)
Abbot Park
Bandrake Head
Ulverston
LA12 8HW
tel 07770 950758
www.abbotpark.co.uk

Crake Valley Campsite (7km off-route)
Lake Bank Water Yeat
Ulverston
LA12 8DL
tel 07741 274546
www.crakevalley.co.uk

YHA Coniston Holly How
Far End Bungalow
Holly How
Coniston
LA21 8DD
tel 0345 371 9511
www.yha.org.uk/hostel/yha-coniston-holly-how

Hoathwaite National Trust Campsite
Near Torver
Coniston
LA21 8AX
tel 015394 32733
www.nationaltrust.org.uk

Coniston to Keswick

Turner Hall Campsite
Seathwaite
Broughton-in-Furness
LA20 6EE
tel 01229 716420
www.turnerhallcampsite.co.uk

Dalegarth Campsite
Dalegarth Hall Cottage
Holmrook
CA19 1TF
tel 07961 281692
https://dalegarthcampsite.co.uk

Bikepacking in the Lake District

Eskdale Campsites Ltd
Holmrook
CA19 1TH

YHA Eskdale
Holmrook
CA19 1TH
tel 0345 371 9317
www.yha.org.uk/hostel/yha-eskdale

Fisherground Campsite
Fellside Cottage
Eskdale
Holmrook
CA19 1TF
tel 019467 23723
www.fishergroundcampsite.co.uk

Eskdale National Trust Campsite
Boot
Holmrook
CA19 1TH
tel 015394 32733
www.nationaltrust.org.uk

The Old Post Office Campsite
(5km off-route)
Santon Bridge
Holmrock
CA19 1UY
tel 019467 26286
www.theoldpostofficecampsite.co.uk

Wasdale National Trust Campsite
Wasdale Head
Seascale
CA20 1EX
tel 015394 32733
www.nationaltrust.org.uk

Seathwaite Farm Camping (4km off-route)
Seathwaite
Keswick
CA12 5XJ
tel 017687 77394
www.seathwaitefarmcamping.co.uk

Inside Out Camping
Seatoller Farm
Borrowdale
Keswick
CA12 5XN
tel 07791 184271
www.insideoutcamping.co.uk

Chapel House Farm Campsite
(2km off-route)
Stonethwaite
Borrowdale
Keswick
CA12 5XG
tel 017687 77256
www.chapelhousefarmcampsite.co.uk

Stonethwaite Farm Campsite
(3km off-route)
Stonethwaite
Keswick
CA12 5XG
tel 017687 77234

Newlands Valley Campsite
Stair
Keswick
CA12 5UE
tel 07495 902051

Appendix A – Lake District campsites and hostels

Lanefoot Farm Campsite (2km off-route)
Thornthwaite
Keswick
CA12 5RZ
tel 017687 78097
www.stayinthornthwaite.co.uk

YHA Black Sail Hut
Ennerdale Bridge
Cleator
CA23 3AX
tel 0345 371 9680
www.yha.org.uk/hostel/yha-black-sail

Keswick to Staveley

Hollows Farm
Grange-in-Borrowdale
Keswick
CA12 5UQ
tel 017687 77298
www.hollowsfarm.co.uk

Derwentwater Camping and
Caravanning Club Site
Crow Park Rd
Keswick
CA12 5EN
tel 017687 72579
www.campingandcaravanningclub.co.uk

Low Briery Holiday Park
Penrith Rd
Keswick
CA12 4RN
tel 017687 72044
www.lowbriery.co.uk

Burns Farm Caravans Camping and
Glamping (2km off-route)
Burns Farm
Keswick
CA12 4RR
tel 017687 79112
www.burns-farm.co.uk

Low Hollows Campsite (2km off-route)
Low Hollows
Threlkeld
Keswick
CA12 4SZ
www.facebook.com/lowhollowcampsite

Lowside Farm Camping (3km off-route)
Lowside Farm
Troutbeck Nr Threlkeld
Penrith
CA11 0SX
tel 017687 75859
www.lowsidefarm.co.uk

Troutbeck Caravan and Camping Park
(4km off-route)
Moor End
Troutbeck
Penrith
CA11 0SX
tel 017687 79149
www.troutbeckcaravanpark.co.uk

Gill Head Farm (5km off-route)
Troutbeck
Penrith
CA11 0ST
tel 017687 79953
www.gillheadfarm.co.uk

Bikepacking in the Lake District

The Quiet Site
Ullswater
Penrith
CA11 0LS
tel 01768 486337
www.thequietsite.co.uk

Waterfoot Caravan Park
Ullswater
Penrith
CA11 0JF
tel 01768 486302
www.waterfootpark.co.uk

Waterside House
Howtown
Penrith
CA10 2NA
tel 01768 486332
www.watersidefarm-campsite.co.uk

Park Foot Holiday Park
Howtown Rd
Pooley Bridge
Penrith
CA10 2NA
tel 01768 486309
www.parkfootullswater.co.uk

Side Farm Campsite
Side Farm
Ullswater
Penrith
CA11 0NL
tel 01768 482337
www.sidefarmcampsite.co.uk

Gillside Farm
Ullswater
Glenridding
Cumbria
CA11 0QQ
tel 017684 82346
www.gillsidecaravanandcampingsite.co.uk

Sykeside Camping Park
and Brotherswater Inn
Brotherswater
Patterdale
Cumbria
CA11 0NZ
tel 01768 482239
www.sykeside.co.uk

Route 2 – The Furness Forests

Witherslack Cycle Barn Bunkhouse
Beck Head
Witherslack
Grange Over Sands
Cumbria
LA11 6SH
tel 015395 52223
www.witherslackcyclebarn.co.uk

Abbots Reading Farm
Haverthwaite
Ulverston
LA12 8JP
tel 07812 173334
www.glampinglakedistrict.com

Appendix A – Lake District campsites and hostels

Black Beck Farm
1 New Hall
Bouth
Ulverston
LA12 8JJ
tel 01229 861284
www.blackbeckfarmholidaycaravans.co.uk

Abbott Park Farm Campsite
(4km off-route)
Abbott Park
Bandrake Head
Ulverston
LA12 8HW
tel 07770 950758
www.abbotpark.co.uk

Grizedale Campsite (1km off-route)
Bowkerstead Farm
Satterthwaite
Ulverston
LA12 8LL
tel 01229 860208
www.grizedale-camping.co.uk

Crake Valley
Lake Bank
Water Yeat
Ulverston
LA12 8DL
tel 01229 885203
www.crakevalley.co.uk

Shepherds View
Torver
Coniston
LA21 8BQ
tel 015394 41239
www.campingandcaravanningclub.co.uk

Hoathwaite National Trust Campsite
Near Torver
Coniston
LA21 8AX
tel 015394 32733
www.nationaltrust.org.uk

Coniston Hall
Cumbria
Coniston
LA21 8AS
tel 015394 41223
https://conistonhallcampsite.co.uk

Glamping at Graythwaite
Cunsey Farm
Ambleside
LA22 0LU
tel 015395 31248
www.graythwaite.com

Bowness-on-Windermere Camping and Caravanning Club
Glebe Rd
Bowness-on-Windermere
Windermere
LA23 3HB
tel 015394 42177
www.campingandcaravanningclub.co.uk

Kendal Camping and Caravanning Club
Millcrest House
Shap Rd
Kendal
LA9 6NY
tel 015397 41363
www.campingandcaravanningclub.co.uk

Bikepacking in the Lake District

Route 3 – The Old Man of Coniston and the Irish Sea

Fisherground Campsite
Fellside Cottage
Eskdale
Holmrook
CA19 1TF
tel 019467 23723
www.fishergroundcampsite.co.uk

Dalegarth Campsite
Dalegarth Hall Cottage
Holmrook
CA19 1TF
tel 07961 281692
https://dalegarthcampsite.co.uk

Eskdale National Trust Campsite
Boot
Holmrook
CA19 1TH
tel 015394 32733
www.nationaltrust.org.uk

YHA Eskdale
Holmrook
CA19 1TH
tel 03453 719317
www.yha.org.uk/hostel/yha-eskdale

Turner Hall Campsite
Seathwaite
Broughton-in-Furness
LA20 6EE
tel 01229 716420
www.turnerhallcampsite.co.uk

Hoathwaite National Trust Campsite
Near Torver
Coniston
LA21 8AX
tel 015394 32733
www.nationaltrust.org.uk

Shepherds View
Torver
Coniston
LA21 8BQ
tel 015394 41239
www.campingandcaravanningclub.co.uk

Hazel Mount Fellside Camping
(1km off-route)
Buckman Brow
Millom
LA18 5JX
tel 07851 197272
www.facebook.com/HMFcamping

Baystone Bank Farm Campsite
Whicham Valley
Millom
LA18 5LY
tel 07456 642155
www.baystonebankfarmcampsite.co.uk

Sturdy Bank Campsite (2km off-route)
Sturdy Bank
Grizebeck
Kirkby-in-Furness
LA17 7XU

Route 4 – Way Out in the Western Fells

Whinfell Hall Farm Campsite
Low Lorton
Cockermouth
CA13 0RQ

Appendix A – Lake District campsites and hostels

tel 07706 976907
www.whinfellcampsite.co.uk

Wheatsheaf Inn Camping
Low Lorton
Cockermouth
CA13 9UW
tel 01900 85199
www.wheatsheafinnlorton.co.uk

Lanefoot Farm Campsite
Thornthwaite
Keswick
CA12 5RZ
www.stayinthornthwaite.co.uk

Syke Farm Campsite
Cockermouth
CA13 9XA
tel 017687 70222
www.sykefarmcampsite.com

Scallow Top
Nursery Rd
Beckermet
CA21 2XB
www.campingandcaravanningclub.co.uk

Seacote Hotel and Holiday Parks
Bay View
2 Rydal
Saint Bees
CA27 0EU
tel 01946 822777
www.seacote.com/seacote-park/tourers-tents

Route 5 – Helvellyn and Back

Bowness-on-Windermere Camping and Caravanning Club Site
Glebe Rd
Bowness-on-Windermere
Windermere
LA23 3HB
tel 015394 42177
www.campingandcaravanningclub.co.uk

Hawkshead Hall Campsite
Ambleside
LA22 0NN
tel 015394 36221
www.hawksheadhall-campsite.co.uk

Baysbrown Farm Campsite
Great Langdale
Ambleside
LA22 9JZ
tel 015394 37150
www.baysbrownfarmcampsite.co.uk

Great Langdale Campsite
The National Trust
Great Langdale
Ambleside
LA22 9JU
tel 015394 32733
www.nationaltrust.org.uk

Side Farm Campsite
Side Farm
Ullswater
Penrith
CA11 0NL
tel 01768 482337
www.sidefarmcampsite.co.uk

Bikepacking in the Lake District

Gillside Farm
Ullswater
Glenridding
Cumbria
CA11 0QQ
tel 017684 82346
www.gillsidecaravanandcampingsite.co.uk

Chapel House Farm
Keswick
CA12 5XG
tel 017687 77256
www.chapelhousefarmcampsite.co.uk

Keswick Camping and
Caravanning Club
Crow Park Rd
Keswick
CA12 5EP
tel 017687 72392
www.campingandcaravanningclub.co.uk

Castlerigg Farm Camping and
Caravan Site (2km off-route)
Castlerigg
Keswick
CA12 4TE
tel 017687 72479
www.castleriggfarm.com

Burns Farm Caravan and Camping
St Johns-in-the-Vale
Keswick
CA12 4RR
tel 017687 79112
www.burns-farm.co.uk

Thirlspot Farm Camping (3km off-route)
Thirlmere
Keswick
CA12 4TN
tel 017687 72551
www.thirlspotfarmcamping.co.uk

High Bridge End Caravan and
Camping Site (4km off-route)
Bridge End Farm
Keswick
CA12 4TG
tel 017687 72166

Dalebottom Farm Campsite
Dalebottom Farm
Naddle
Keswick
CA12 4TF
tel 017687 74713
www.dalebottomfarm.co.uk

Rydal Hall Campsite
Rydal Hall
1 The Croft
Rydal
Ambleside
LA22 9LX
tel 015394 32050
www.rydalhall.org

Route 6 – Dalston/Skiddaw Mega Pretzel

Camping at Cardewlees
Cardewlees Farm
Dalston
Carlisle
CA5 6LF

Appendix A – Lake District campsites and hostels

tel 07958 195852
www.campingatcardewlees.com

Thornfield Camping Cabins En-suite
Glamping Pods with Hot Tubs
Hawksdale
Dalston
Carlisle
CA5 7BX
tel 01228 319028
www.thornfieldcampingcabins.co.uk

Pasturewood Holidays (2km off-route)
Dalston
Carlisle
CA5 7DR
tel 07898 282615
www.pasturewoodholidays.co.uk

Fellhill Pods Glamping Pods
Fell Hill Farm
Carlisle
CA5 7HH
tel 016974 78257
www.fellhillpods.co.uk

Caldbeck Camping
Mill View
Friar Row
Caldbeck
Wigton
CA7 8DS
tel 016974 78367
www.caldbeckcamping.co.uk

Kestrel Lodge Campsite
Bassenthwaite
Keswick
CA12 4QX

tel 017687 76752
www.kestrellodge.co.uk

Skiddaw House
Bassenthwaite
Keswick
CA12 4QX
tel 07747 174293
www.yha.org.uk/hostel/yha-skiddaw-bunkhouse

Lingy Hut (bothy on the route below summit of Great Lingy Hill)
Keswick
CA12 4QX

Low Hollows
Threlkeld
Keswick
CA12 4SZ
www.facebook.com/lowhollowcampsite

Lowside Farm
Troutbeck
Nr Threlkeld
Penrith
CA11 0SX
tel 017687 75859
www.lowsidefarm.co.uk

Troutbeck Caravan and Camping Park
Moor End
Troutbeck
Penrith
CA11 0SX
tel 017687 79149
www.troutbeckcaravanpark.co.uk

Bikepacking in the Lake District

Gill Head Farm
Troutbeck
Penrith
CA11 0ST
tel 017687 79953
www.gillheadfarm.co.uk

Carrock Glamping Pods
Linewath
Hesket Newmarket
Wigton
CA7 8JT
tel 07770 551177
www.carrockpods.co.uk

Route 7 – Penrith/High Street Circuit

Setterah Park Farm Campsite
Setterah Park Farm
Helton
Penrith
CA10 2QB
tel 01931 712593
https://setterahpark.wixsite.com/setterahparkcampsite

Croft House Campsite
Croft House
Rosgill
Bampton
Penrith
CA10 2QX
tel 01931 717431
www.ukcampsite.co.uk

High Borrans Lodges
Windermere
LA23 1JS
tel 015394 43313
www.windermere-lodge.com

Kentmere Farm Pods
Browfoot Farm
Brow Foot Ln
Kendal
LA8 9JQ
tel 01539 821210
www.farmpods.co.uk

YHA Windermere
Bridge Ln
Troutbeck Bridge
Windermere
LA23 1LA
tel 0345 371 9352
www.yha.org.uk/hostel/yha-windermere

Troutbeck Camping Pods
High Kingate
Troutbeck
Windermere
LA23 1PN
tel 07891 634592
www.troutbeckcampingpods.co.uk

Camp Eden
Lowther Castle
Lowther
CA10 2HH
www.campeden.co.uk

Route 8 – Nine Lakes

As route covers most of Lakeland, see Lakeland 200 or other routes.

Appendix B
Lake District bike shops

Ghyllside Cycles
The Slack
Ambleside
LA22 9DQ
tel 015394 33592
www.ghyllside.co.uk

PUSH Cartel
North Rd
Ambleside
LA22 9DT
tel 015394 31408
www.pushcartel.co.uk

Alpkit Ambleside (outdoor equipment)
100 Lake Rd
Ambleside
LA22 0DB
tel 015394 54954
www.alpkit.com/pages/ambleside

Biketreks Grizedale
Grizedale Forest
Ambleside
LA22 0QJ
tel 015394 31245
www.bike-treks.co.uk

Biketreks Ings
Ings
Kendal
LA8 9PY
tel 015394 31245
www.bike-treks.co.uk

Wheelbase Cycles
Staveley Mill Yard
Back Ln
Staveley
Kendal
LA8 9LR
tel 01539 821443
www.wheelbase.co.uk/about-us/our-stores/wheelbase-lake-district/

Country Lanes Cycle Centre
Windermere Railway Station
Station Precinct
Windermere
LA23 1AH
tel 015394 44544
www.countrylaneslakedistrict.co.uk

Summitreks (outdoor equipment, not a bike shop)
5 Yewdale Rd
Coniston
LA21 8DU
tel 015394 41822
www.summitreks.co.uk

Keswick Bikes Ltd
133 Main St
Keswick
CA12 5NJ
tel 017687 75202
www.keswickbikes.co.uk

E-Venture Bikes Lake District
The Hub
Elliott Park
Keswick
Cumbria
tel 017687 21920
www.e-venturebikes.co.uk

Bikepacking in the Lake District

Whinlatter Bikes
82 Main St
Keswick
CA12 5DX
tel 017687 73940
www.whinlatterbikes.com

Arragons Cycle Hire
Lowther Castle
Penrith
CA10 2HH
tel 01768 890344
www.arragonscyclehire.com

Cyclewise
Whinlatter Forest Visitor Centre
near Braithwaite
CA12 5TW
tel 017687 78711
www.cyclewise.co.uk

Scotby Cycles
Church St
Carlisle
CA2 5TL
www.scotbycycles.co.uk

Haven Cycles
Preston St
Whitehaven
CA28 9DL
tel 01946 63263
www.havencycles-c2cservices.co.uk

Ainfield Cycle Centre
Jacktrees Rd
Cleator
CA23 3DW
tel 01946 812427
www.ainfieldcycles.co.uk

4 Play Cycles
25–31 Market Pl
Cockermouth
CA13 9NH
tel 01900 823377
www.4playcycles.co.uk

Appendix C
Kit list

Essential kit list

(if depending on local facilities for food and a campsite)

Clothes
- Padded shorts
- Off-road cycling shoes
- Trainers or trail shoes
- Two pairs of suitable socks
- Long-sleeved top
- Short-sleeved top
- Waterproof jacket
- Helmet

Repair kit
- Two inner tubes for your tyres
- Tyre levers
- Multitool
- Chain tool and spare link
- Puncture repair kit
- Pump

Camping equipment
- Tent or bivvy bag
- Sleeping bag
- Sleeping mat
- Head torch (including spare batteries if required)

Other
- Water bottle(s)
- First aid kit (including antiseptic wipes and plasters)
- Mobile phone (to provide alternative means of navigation)
- Lights (to see by and be seen by)
- Spare battery for lights
- Power pack to charge lights and phone
- Electrolytes
- Toilet roll
- Light shovel
- Map
- Compass
- Micro-rucksack

Extended list

(if going out of season/being fully self-supported)

Clothes
- Waterproof gloves
- Waterproof socks
- Warm hat
- Arm warmers
- Thermal leggings
- Down jacket/synthetic down jacket
- Full-length padded leggings
- Snood

Repair kit
- Spare chain/quick-link
- Spare tyre
- CO_2 gas canisters and dispenser
- Oil
- Rag

Other
- Cycling computer
- Backup power pack
- Tarp and hammock set up
- Gas stove
- Pot
- Mug
- Coffee equipment/coffee
- Food for the duration
- Water filter
- Camping knife/Leatherman
- Flint lighter (matches might get wet)
- Long spork
- Dry bags
- Cash

Notes

Download the routes in GPX Format

All the routes in this guide are available for download from:

www.cicerone.co.uk/1117/GPX

as standard format GPX files. You should be able to load them into most online GPX systems and mobile devices, whether GPS or smartphone. You may need to convert the file into your preferred format using a conversion programme such as gpsvisualizer.com or one of the many other such websites and programmes.

When you follow this link, you will be asked for your email address and where you purchased the guidebook, and have the option to subscribe to the Cicerone e-newsletter.

www.cicerone.co.uk

Listing of Cicerone guides

BRITISH ISLES CHALLENGES, COLLECTIONS AND ACTIVITIES

Cycling Land's End to John o' Groats
Great Walks on the England Coast Path
The Big Rounds
The Book of the Bivvy
The Book of the Bothy
The Mountains of England & Wales:
  Vol 1 Wales
  Vol 2 England
The National Trails
Walking the End to End Trail
short walks series
Short Walks Hadrian's Wall
Short Walks in Arnside and Silverdale
Short Walks in Dumfries and Galloway
Short Walks in Nidderdale
Short Walks in the Lake District: Windermere Ambleside and Grasmere
Short Walks on the Malvern Hills
Short Walks in the Surrey Hills
Short Walks Winchester

SCOTLAND

Ben Nevis and Glen Coe
Cycle Touring in Northern Scotland
Cycling in the Hebrides
Great Mountain Days in Scotland
Mountain Biking in Southern and Central Scotland
Mountain Biking in West and North West Scotland
Not the West Highland Way
Scotland
Scotland's Best Small Mountains
Scotland's Mountain Ridges
Scottish Wild Country Backpacking
Skye's Cuillin Ridge Traverse
The Borders Abbeys Way
The Great Glen Way
The Great Glen Way Map Booklet
The Hebridean Way
The Hebrides
The Isle of Mull
The Isle of Skye
The Skye Trail
The Southern Upland Way
The West Highland Way
The West Highland Way Map Booklet

Walking Ben Lawers, Rannoch and Atholl
Walking in the Cairngorms
Walking in the Pentland Hills
Walking in the Scottish Borders
Walking in the Southern Uplands
Walking in Torridon, Fisherfield, Fannichs and An Teallach
Walking Loch Lomond and the Trossachs
Walking on Arran
Walking on Harris and Lewis
Walking on Jura, Islay and Colonsay
Walking on Rum and the Small Isles
Walking on the Orkney and Shetland Isles
Walking on Uist and Barra
Walking the Cape Wrath Trail
Walking the Corbetts
  Vol 1 South of the Great Glen
  Vol 2 North of the Great Glen
Walking the Galloway Hills
Walking the John o' Groats Trail
Walking the Munros
  Vol 1 – Southern, Central and Western Highlands
  Vol 2 – Northern Highlands and the Cairngorms
Winter Climbs: Ben Nevis and Glen Coe

NORTHERN ENGLAND ROUTES

Cycling the Reivers Route
Cycling the Way of the Roses
Hadrian's Cycleway
Hadrian's Wall Path
Hadrian's Wall Path Map Booklet
The Coast to Coast Cycle Route
The Coast to Coast Walk
The Coast to Coast Walk Map Booklet
The Pennine Way
The Pennine Way Map Booklet
Walking the Dales Way
Walking the Dales Way Map Booklet

NORTH-EAST ENGLAND, YORKSHIRE DALES AND PENNINES

Cycling in the Yorkshire Dales
Great Mountain Days in the Pennines
Mountain Biking in the Yorkshire Dales
The Cleveland Way and the Yorkshire Wolds Way
The Cleveland Way Map Booklet
The North York Moors
The Reivers Way
Trail and Fell Running in the Yorkshire Dales
Walking in County Durham
Walking in Northumberland
Walking in the North Pennines

Walking in the Yorkshire Dales: North and East
Walking in the Yorkshire Dales: South and West
Walking St Cuthbert's Way
Walking St Oswald's Way and Northumberland Coast Path

NORTH-WEST ENGLAND AND THE ISLE OF MAN

Cycling the Pennine Bridleway
Isle of Man Coastal Path
The Lancashire Cycleway
The Lune Valley and Howgills
Walking in Cumbria's Eden Valley
Walking in Lancashire
Walking in the Forest of Bowland and Pendle
Walking on the Isle of Man
Walking on the West Pennine Moors
Walking the Ribble Way
Walks in Silverdale and Arnside

LAKE DISTRICT

Bikepacking in the Lake District
Cycling in the Lake District
Great Mountain Days in the Lake District
Joss Naylor's Lakes, Meres and Waters of the Lake District
Lake District Winter Climbs
Lake District: High Level and Fell Walks
Lake District: Low Level and Lake Walks
Mountain Biking in the Lake District
Outdoor Adventures with Children – Lake District
Scrambles in the Lake District – North
Scrambles in the Lake District – South
Trail and Fell Running in the Lake District
Walking The Cumbria Way
Walking the Lake District Fells –
  Borrowdale
  Buttermere
  Coniston
  Keswick
  Langdale
  Mardale and the Far East
  Patterdale
  Wasdale
Walking the Tour of the Lake District

DERBYSHIRE, PEAK DISTRICT AND MIDLANDS

Cycling in the Peak District
Dark Peak Walks
Scrambles in the Dark Peak
Walking in Derbyshire
Walking in the Peak District – White Peak East
Walking in the Peak District – White Peak West

SOUTHERN ENGLAND

20 Classic Sportive Rides in South East England
20 Classic Sportive Rides in South West England
Cycling in the Cotswolds
Mountain Biking on the North Downs
Mountain Biking on the South Downs
Suffolk Coast and Heath Walks
The Cotswold Way
The Cotswold Way Map Booklet
The Kennet and Avon Canal
The Lea Valley Walk
The North Downs Way
The North Downs Way Map Booklet
The Peddars Way and Norfolk Coast Path
The Pilgrims' Way
The Ridgeway National Trail
The Ridgeway National Trail Map Booklet
The South Downs Way
The South Downs Way Map Booklet
The Thames Path
The Thames Path Map Booklet
The Two Moors Way
The Two Moors Way Map Booklet
Walking Hampshire's Test Way
Walking in Cornwall
Walking in Essex
Walking in Kent
Walking in London
Walking in Norfolk
Walking in the Chilterns
Walking in the Cotswolds
Walking in the Isles of Scilly
Walking in the New Forest
Walking in the North Wessex Downs
Walking on Dartmoor
Walking on Guernsey
Walking on Jersey
Walking on the Isle of Wight
Walking the Dartmoor Way
Walking the Jurassic Coast
Walking the South West Coast Path
Walking the South West Coast Path Map Booklets
 – Vol 1: Minehead to St Ives
 – Vol 2: St Ives to Plymouth
 – Vol 3: Plymouth to Poole
Walks in the South Downs National Park

WALES AND WELSH BORDERS

Cycle Touring in Wales
Cycling Lon Las Cymru
Glyndwr's Way
Great Mountain Days in Snowdonia
Hillwalking in Shropshire
Mountain Walking in Snowdonia
Offa's Dyke Path
Offa's Dyke Path Map Booklet
Ridges of Snowdonia
Scrambles in Snowdonia
Snowdonia: 30 Low-level and Easy Walks – North
Snowdonia: 30 Low-level and Easy Walks – South
The Cambrian Way
The Pembrokeshire Coast Path
The Pembrokeshire Coast Path Map Booklet
The Snowdonia Way
The Wye Valley Walk
Walking in Carmarthenshire
Walking in Pembrokeshire
Walking in the Brecon Beacons
Walking in the Forest of Dean
Walking in the Wye Valley
Walking on Gower
Walking the Severn Way
Walking the Shropshire Way
Walking the Wales Coast Path

INTERNATIONAL CHALLENGES, COLLECTIONS AND ACTIVITIES

Europe's High Points
Walking the Via Francigena Pilgrim Route – Part 1

AFRICA

Kilimanjaro
Walking in the Drakensberg
Walks and Scrambles in the Moroccan Anti-Atlas

ALPS CROSS-BORDER ROUTES

100 Hut Walks in the Alps
Alpine Ski Mountaineering Vol 1 – Western Alps
The Karnischer Hohenweg
The Tour of the Bernina
Trail Running – Chamonix and the Mont Blanc region
Trekking Chamonix to Zermatt
Trekking in the Alps
Trekking in the Silvretta and Ratikon Alps
Trekking Munich to Venice
Trekking the Tour of Mont Blanc
Walking in the Alps

PYRENEES AND FRANCE/SPAIN CROSS-BORDER ROUTES

Shorter Treks in the Pyrenees
The GR11 Trail
The Pyrenean Haute Route
The Pyrenees
Walks and Climbs in the Pyrenees

AUSTRIA

Innsbruck Mountain Adventures
Trekking Austria's Adlerweg
Trekking in Austria's Hohe Tauern
Trekking in Austria's Zillertal Alps
Trekking in the Stubai Alps
Walking in Austria
Walking in the Salzkammergut: the Austrian Lake District

EASTERN EUROPE

The Danube Cycleway Vol 2
The Elbe Cycle Route
The High Tatras
The Mountains of Romania
Walking in Hungary

FRANCE, BELGIUM AND LUXEMBOURG

Camino de Santiago – Via Podiensis
Chamonix Mountain Adventures
Cycle Touring in France
Cycling London to Paris
Cycling the Canal de la Garonne
Cycling the Canal du Midi
Cycling the Route des Grandes Alpes
Mont Blanc Walks
Mountain Adventures in the Maurienne
Short Treks on Corsica
The GR5 Trail
The GR5 Trail – Benelux and Lorraine
The GR5 Trail – Vosges and Jura
The Grand Traverse of the Massif Central
The Moselle Cycle Route
The River Loire Cycle Route
The River Rhone Cycle Route
Trekking in the Vanoise
Trekking the Cathar Way
Trekking the GR10
Trekking the GR20 Corsica
Trekking the Robert Louis Stevenson Trail
Via Ferratas of the French Alps
Walking in Provence – East
Walking in Provence – West
Walking in the Ardennes
Walking in the Auvergne
Walking in the Brianconnais
Walking in the Dordogne
Walking in the Haute Savoie: North
Walking in the Haute Savoie: South
Walking on Corsica
Walking the Brittany Coast Path

GERMANY

Hiking and Cycling in the Black Forest
The Danube Cycleway Vol 1
The Rhine Cycle Route
The Westweg
Walking in the Bavarian Alps

IRELAND
The Wild Atlantic Way and Western Ireland
Walking the Wicklow Way

ITALY
Alta Via 1 – Trekking in the Dolomites
Alta Via 2 – Trekking in the Dolomites
Day Walks in the Dolomites
Italy's Grande Traversata delle Alpi
Italy's Sibillini National Park
Ski Touring and Snowshoeing in the Dolomites
The Way of St Francis
Trekking in the Apennines
Trekking the Giants' Trail: Alta Via 1 through the Italian Pennine Alps
Via Ferratas of the Italian Dolomites Vols 1&2
Walking and Trekking in the Gran Paradiso
Walking in Abruzzo
Walking in Italy's Cinque Terre
Walking in Italy's Stelvio National Park
Walking in Sicily
Walking in the Aosta Valley
Walking in the Dolomites
Walking in Tuscany
Walking in Umbria
Walking Lake Como and Maggiore
Walking Lake Garda and Iseo
Walking on the Amalfi Coast
Walking the Via Francigena Pilgrim Route – Parts 2&3
Walks and Treks in the Maritime Alps

MEDITERRANEAN
The High Mountains of Crete
Trekking in Greece
Walking and Trekking in Zagori
Walking and Trekking on Corfu
Walking in Cyprus
Walking on Malta
Walking on the Greek Islands – the Cyclades

NEW ZEALAND AND AUSTRALIA
Hiking the Overland Track

NORTH AMERICA
Hiking and Cycling the California Missions Trail
The John Muir Trail
The Pacific Crest Trail

SOUTH AMERICA
Aconcagua and the Southern Andes
Hiking and Biking Peru's Inca Trails
Trekking in Torres del Paine

SCANDINAVIA, ICELAND AND GREENLAND
Hiking in Norway – South
Trekking in Greenland – The Arctic Circle Trail
Trekking the Kungsleden
Walking and Trekking in Iceland

SLOVENIA, CROATIA, SERBIA, MONTENEGRO AND ALBANIA
Hiking Slovenia's Juliana Trail
Mountain Biking in Slovenia
The Islands of Croatia
The Julian Alps of Slovenia
The Mountains of Montenegro
The Peaks of the Balkans Trail
The Slovene Mountain Trail
Walking in Slovenia: The Karavanke
Walks and Treks in Croatia

SPAIN AND PORTUGAL
Camino de Santiago: Camino Frances
Coastal Walks in Andalucia
Costa Blanca Mountain Adventures
Cycling the Camino de Santiago
Cycling the Ruta Via de la Plata
Mountain Walking in Mallorca
Mountain Walking in Southern Catalunya
Portugal's Rota Vicentina
Spain's Sendero Historico: The GR1
The Andalucian Coast to Coast Walk
The Camino del Norte and Camino Primitivo
The Camino Ingles and Ruta do Mar
The Camino Portugues
The Mountains of Nerja
The Mountains of Ronda and Grazalema
The Sierras of Extremadura
Trekking in Mallorca
Trekking in the Canary Islands
Trekking the GR7 in Andalucia
Walking and Trekking in the Sierra Nevada
Walking in Andalucia
Walking in Catalunya – Barcelona
Walking in Catalunya – Girona Pyrenees
Walking in Portugal
Walking in the Algarve
Walking in the Picos de Europa
Walking on Gran Canaria
Walking on La Gomera and El Hierro
Walking on La Palma
Walking on Lanzarote and Fuerteventura
Walking on Madeira
Walking on Tenerife
Walking on the Azores
Walking on the Costa Blanca
Walking the Camino dos Faros

SWITZERLAND
Switzerland's Jura Crest Trail
The Swiss Alps
Tour of the Jungfrau Region
Trekking the Swiss Via Alpina
Walking in the Bernese Oberland – Jungfrau region
Walking in the Engadine – Switzerland
Walking in the Valais
Walking in Ticino
Walking in Zermatt and Saas-Fee

CHINA, JAPAN AND ASIA
Hiking and Trekking in the Japan Alps and Mount Fuji
Hiking in Hong Kong
Japan's Kumano Kodo Pilgrimage
Trekking in Tajikistan

HIMALAYA
Annapurna
Everest: A Trekker's Guide
Trekking in Bhutan
Trekking in Ladakh
Trekking in the Himalaya

MOUNTAIN LITERATURE
8000 metres
A Walk in the Clouds
Abode of the Gods
Fifty Years of Adventure
The Pennine Way – the Path, the People, the Journey
Unjustifiable Risk?

TECHNIQUES
Fastpacking
Geocaching in the UK
Map and Compass
Outdoor Photography
The Mountain Hut Book

MINI GUIDES
Alpine Flowers
Navigation
Pocket First Aid and Wilderness Medicine
Snow

For full information on all our guides, books and eBooks, visit our website:
www.cicerone.co.uk

CICERONE

Trust Cicerone to guide your next adventure, wherever it may be around the world...

Discover guides for hiking, mountain walking, backpacking, trekking, trail running, cycling and mountain biking, ski touring, climbing and scrambling in Britain, Europe and worldwide.

Connect with Cicerone online and find inspiration.

- buy books and ebooks
- articles, advice and trip reports
- podcasts and live events
- GPX files and updates
- regular newsletter

cicerone.co.uk